A DEADLY INNOCENCE

Previous books by the same author

The Defender, 1980
Glasgow: a Celebration (Contributor), 1984
Tales of the Suspected, 1988

A DEADLY INNOCENCE

JOE BELTRAMI

MAINSTREAM
PUBLISHING

First published in Great Britain 1989 by
MAINSTREAM PUBLISHING COMPANY (EDINBURGH) LTD
7 Albany Street
Edinburgh EH1 3UG
ISBN 1 85158 297 5 (cloth)

British Library Cataloguing in Publication Data
Beltrami, Joseph
    A deadly innocence: the Meehan file.
    1. Scotland. Strathclyde Region. Ayr. Ross, Rachel. Murder. Trial of Meehan,
Patrick
    I. Title
    344.1105'2523'0924

    ISBN 1-85158-297-5

Typeset in Palatino by C. R. Barber & Partners Ltd, Fort William
Printed in Great Britain by Richard Clay Ltd, Bungay

Dedicated to my wife, Delia.

Studio Four

I would like to express my thanks to the following persons who have assisted me in the course of the preparation of this book.

My wife Delia, my sons Adrian and Jason, Nicky Fairbairn, the Clerk of Justiciary, Bill Dunlop, Advocate and last but by no means least, Bill Allsopp.

CONTENTS

A DEADLY INNOCENCE
BY
JOSEPH BELTRAMI

In the early hours of 6 July 1969, two raiders
broke into the home of Mr and Mrs Abraham Ross,
in Blackburn Place, Ayr, while they
lay sleeping. Mr and Mrs Ross were both
assaulted during the robbery.

The raiders left the elderly couple injured and
bound, and by the time they were found
72-year-old Mrs Rachel Ross was dying.

It was a callous but, in many respects, an
unremarkable crime—except that murder hunt
detectives decided within days of Mrs Rachel Ross's
death that two small-time crooks, Patrick Meehan
and Jim Griffiths, were responsible.

Meehan was arrested—and Griffiths was shot
dead by a police marksman, after a running
battle across the West End of Glasgow.

Meehan's arrest, conviction and life imprisonment
for murder was to begin a 15-year struggle by
Glasgow criminal lawyer, Joseph Beltrami, to
prove that his client was innocent.
And along the way more people were to die . . .

FOREWORD

by

William Allsopp

This is a story about Glasgow, about its violent underworld of criminals and gangsters—but, above all, about a lawyer's fight for 15 years to prove a man innocent of murder.

Not many successful, well-established criminal lawyers would do what Joe Beltrami did—leave the safety and comfort of their penthouse offices and dip into a city's seedy world of murderous 'hard men', robbers, safe-blowers, thieves, petty crooks and conmen, to find evidence to clear a client.

In *A Deadly Innocence* Joe Beltrami tells, for the first time, of his personal experiences while proving that small-time safe-blower and thief Paddy Meehan could not have murdered 72-year-old Mrs Rachel Ross in her bungalow home during a burglary in 1969.

For Beltrami, it was an uphill battle against the police, the legal system and, in the end, the British establishment. For seven years he virtually lost every battle. His client was jailed for life for murder and was sent to Peterhead Prison.

But Joe Beltrami didn't give up. His belief in Meehan's innocence kept him going. His real horror that the Scottish legal system, which he so admired, was sustaining an injustice, kept him going.

And, of course, his determination to prove his case to those who scoffed and sneered at his single-minded campaign sustained him, too. Beltrami's pride is as powerful a factor as his professional skills in winning cases in the courtroom.

As a journalist working in Glasgow throughout the 'sixties and 'seventies, I had often watched Joe Beltrami instruct counsel as criminal defence lawyer in cases before the High Court of Justiciary.

In the courtroom he was the link between the murky world of criminal dishonesty and brutality, and the carefully ordered and douce world of law-abiding respectability.

I often speculated about some kind of culture-warp that he must undergo. I wondered—What did this big, gruff, intense-looking man think of these people he had as clients? How did he deal with them, handle them? Just how *involved* was he with this underworld? What tales could he tell?

The Meehan Case was to raise even more intriguing questions.

Over the years, Joe Beltrami had certainly built up some kind of relationship with the underworld of Glasgow. He was a successful defence lawyer and much of his clientèle was to come from the criminal class. Many were beholden to him for their extended freedom, won in the courtroom, or for mitigated penalties. Certainly, they sought him out constantly when in trouble with the law.

The underworld owed Beltrami many a debt—although, by its nature, it was not organised enough, or sentimental enough, or gracious enough, to articulate something like this.

Until the Paddy Meehan case, that is. . . .

There is reason to believe that powerful members of the underworld became aware of Joe Beltrami's distress at failing to convince the legal system of Meehan's innocence. They knew of the scoffers. They knew of the indignities and rebukes that he was suffering at the hands of that legal system.

The underworld also came to know how the real murderer 'confessed' to Beltrami, but within the bounds of solicitor-client confidentiality—thus hog-tying him with a terrible secret.

And, of course, in desperation, had not Joe Beltrami himself appealed to that same underworld for some reassurance that he was right? The fact that one of their kind was allowing another to be in prison for a murder he did not commit may also have disturbed some underworld code.

But did the underworld, or some powerful member of it, order the murder of 'Tank' McGuinness, the actual murderer of Mrs Ross? And was the murderer of McGuinness murdered, too, on the order of an underworld Mr Big? Was the second accomplice in the murder of Mrs Ross—Ian Waddell—also murdered by the underworld?

What is true is that four men linked with the Ayr murder all died violent deaths. This is the 'deadliness' of Paddy Meehan's innocence.

At one stage, even Joe Beltrami was reported to the police as having a hand in the murder of his tormentor, McGuinness. This, of course, Beltrami dismisses as preposterous. He does concede that some kind of pressure was put on McGuinness by the underworld to confess and allow Meehan to be freed.

There was even a time when Beltrami looked to the security of his own home, fearful that someone contemplated violence against him, and for three years, while he lived with the secret of who the real killers were, this menace was always present.

This was the Glasgow of the 'seventies. Glasgow of the 'eighties has not changed that much, for all its 1990 status as European City of Culture, for all its 'Merchant City' trendiness and city centre entrepreneurs. Glasgow still has its sub-culture of crime and violence— and its underworld still turns to Joe Beltrami to defend it against criminal charges in the courtroom.

Joe Beltrami protests that, as a criminal defence lawyer, it is not his place to act as judge and jury—only to represent his clients, whoever they are, as they plead in the courts. And accused persons should be judged purely on the evidence given and within the rules of the law. He also warns that the presumption of innocence must begin long before that stage.

Even as this manuscript was being offered to the publishers Joe Beltrami tells how, at a gathering of the Scottish legal establishment, he was told: 'Look around this room—50 per cent of the people here still think Meehan was as guilty as sin.'

Beltrami trusts that A Deadly Innocence can persuade many who still hold that opinion that they are wrong—and dangerously so.

William Allsopp was a reporter and feature writer with the Scottish Daily Express *and* Sunday Times *from 1956–1976. He is now Lecturer in Journalism at Napier Polytechnic of Edinburgh.*

PROLOGUE

by

Sir Nicholas Fairbairn QC, MP

No case in the terrible lexicon of murder has produced so many subsidiary and interlocking deaths as the murder of Mrs Rachel Ross in her home off Racecourse Road, Ayr, in July 1969. Indeed almost all the principal participants in the Meehan saga are dead. Among the few exceptions are the author of this book and the writer of this addendum.

And, strangest and most ironic of all, Patrick Connelly Meehan, who was indicted for the murder of Mrs Ross, and thereafter wrongly and most wrongously convicted, is still alive—pardoned and free. For had death by hanging still been the mandatory penalty for murder, his name unquestionably would have been added to the long roll of those connected with this case who ended their days by death, natural or otherwise.

In this case, too, for the first time ever, there was an application before the three most senior Scottish judges to have evidence taken under the truth drug. This application was summarily refused by the senior judges, Lord Cameron sardonically observing that it was the duty of the Court to protect accused persons from the 'folly' of their legal advisors.

Certainly, the trial judge, Lord Grant, determinedly and irascibly drew the jury's attention to the 'folly' of his legal advisors and successfully frustrated the defence which they presented on his behalf, which, more than anything, resulted in Meehan's wrongful conviction.

However, it was the same legal advisors and their persistent 'folly' which obtained, eventually but tardily, his pardon for wrongful conviction seven years later.

The Appeal Court subsequently refused Meehan's appeal, and all Meehan's appeals and applications to prosecute members of the police by Bills of Criminal Letters were stoutly refused by the Court.

It took the death of one of the actual murderers, William 'Tank' McGuinness, to shake open finally the gates of Meehan's cell. McGuinness was a violent criminal, who was himself murdered in the streets of Glasgow. Fortunately, his widow and family immediately fulfilled his request and reported all his confessions to the Ross murder to the author of this book, Mr Beltrami, to whom McGuinness had, from time to time, given similar information.

Mr Beltrami applied to the Law Society of Scotland for the waiving of confidentiality between lawyer and client—as his client was now dead—*but Mr Beltrami still has not received the answer to these communings.*

Nevertheless, Mr Beltrami went on to reveal his late client's communications, to him and his own family, to the Crown authorities.

The new Secretary of State for Scotland, Bruce Millan, ordained that justice must be done and, regardless of past opposition, courageously ordered and insisted that Meehan should be pardoned.

The Secretary of State also set up another enquiry, under the renowned Court of Session judge, Lord Hunter, whose duty was to investigate all aspects of the matter, including the conduct of the Lord Advocate and associated matters.

In flat contradiction of the authority of Parliament, Lord Hunter constructed a shaky, far-fetched and fatuous surmise as to how Meehan and Griffiths were somehow involved, as well as, and along with, Waddell and McGuinness.

Never was it suggested before or during the trial, or by the two Rosses, or any witness, that other than two malefactors were involved in the crime. Thus, for the final twist, the last attempt by the establishment to try to bring Meehan yet once more into the frame. This attempt was to be singularly unsuccessful and, indeed, the whole report was excluded from the mind of the person requested by Parliament to quantify Meehan's damages.

There, then, is the synopsis of this tapestry of inter-woven irony, paradox, infamy and death, in this story about justice.

This whole amazing tale, with all its implications for right and wrong, and for good and evil, is told in this account with fascinating clarity and engaging enthusiasm by the man who was involved in his professional capacity in every episode of this extraordinary saga. But for his unbounded energy in pursuit of justice and freedom for an innocent man who was wrongly convicted, that man would still be serving a sentence for a crime he did not commit.

From this tale, nevertheless, there emerge two survivors—Meehan and justice. I say this because it is just that of all those involved, death has escaped the innocent central figure of Meehan who, a few years before, would have been hanged. And how much more difficult it would have been then, to establish his innocence.

I ask one final question: Is it not the case that not even a word of censure, far less dismissal or prosecution, has visited a single person who may have been responsible for bringing about and sustaining Meehan's wrongful conviction and prolonged imprisonment?

The purpose of this book must be for those in charge of the machinery of justice to search not only in their consciences but their souls.

INTRODUCTION

by

Joe Beltrami

'. . . few are concerned to clear the innocent.'

What you are about to read requires to be publicised in order to ensure that a number of facts of this celebrated case of Patrick Connelly Meehan, unique as these are, should not disappear in the passage of time.

There are also lessons to be learned by us all, irrespective of our station in life. As Daniel Defoe once put it, 'I hear much of people's calling out to punish the guilty, but very few are concerned to clear the innocent.'

Unique this case must surely be. After seven years in Peterhead Prison, having been sentenced to life imprisonment in 1969, Meehan was granted a Royal Pardon on 19 May 1976—the first and only dispensed in Scotland this century following a murder conviction.

Having practised criminal law during the 17 years prior to 1973, I felt that my experience at that time would be capable of seeing me through most tricky situations which could possibly confront me, and with more than a little to spare. After all, had I not represented more people charged with murder than any other solicitor in the country?

Had I not given evidence on a number of occasions at High and

Lower court level, acted in many capital and non-capital murder trials, and taken many unusual appeals, occasionally making new law?

And had I not been instructed in connection with every conceivable crime in the book—not to mention courts-martial at home and abroad—interviewed literally thousands of witnesses and accused persons, and attended more identification parades than I cared to remember?

Yet I could not envisage a situation which would drive me to such despair and leave me so frustrated. How utterly wrong I was! My undoubted confidence in my ability to cope overall had been built on sand.

I concede this in the knowledge that some of the facts that I shall narrate are such that no solicitor in this land can ever possibly have been called upon to face. Indeed, what was to follow the eventful month of January 1973 was a scenario one would have thought only MGM or United Artists could conjure up. However, this was no celluloid fantasy—this was a situation that was very, very real.

1

During the year of 1973, and frequently in the next two years, a murderer would appear in my office, always unannounced, never by appointment, and he would see only me. He would sit across the desk from me, tormenting me—although, in fairness, this was not his purpose—with more and more of his dark and dramatic secret.

He and another man had been responsible for the murder of an elderly Jewish woman during a robbery at her bungalow home some four years earlier. Neither of them had been caught, although the man in front of me had escaped capture by the proverbial whisker. Now, here he was, sitting in my office as a client, slowly dripping more and more information that an innocent man, Patrick Meehan, had been jailed for that murder.

Indeed, he was saying more than that . . . he was virtually telling me that *he* was the murderer.

And I was helpless! Because of a strict rule of confidentiality between solicitor and client, I could do nothing about it—while Meehan, also a client of mine, languished in jail.

Call it, if you will, a golden rule that cannot be broken, rather like that of a confessor in the Roman Catholic church. He, too, can never divulge anything told to him within the walls of the confessional. For three years I was well and truly saddled with the crushing burden of knowing that such confidences between solicitor and client are inviolable *for the lifetime of the client*.

This man, who had been a client of mine on and off since the early 'sixties, was William 'Tank' McGuinness—a small, thin, almost skeletal

Glasgow 'hard man'. He stood barely five feet six inches and must have weighed scarcely more than eight-and-a-half stones, and, at the time of those memorable meetings, he was in his mid-forties.

'Tank' had a marked perennial pallor, with protruding cheek bones serving to exaggerate sunken cheeks. He often wore two pairs of trousers because he felt the cold more than most, due to some circulatory complaint. Steely blue eyes were his only outstanding feature. His eyes did not just look at you—they looked through you. And his face was patterned with scars—mementos, no doubt, of his violent and explosive past.

There was an air of menace about 'Tank' McGuinness, a Glaswegian of some criminal renown. He was a ruthless, evil-tempered and often unstable criminal, feared by many—and with good reason. As well as being a hardened criminal, he had all the hallmarks of a confirmed psychopath, who knew little of the meaning of fear or conscience.

He was a man of few words and limited vocabulary, and was extremely soft-spoken. From time to time one could trace a not-too-pronounced impediment as he struggled with certain words. If anything, he was inclined to mumble. I found his constant staring more than a little off-putting and, as he sat opposite me, I was often ill-at-ease.

In his favour, he was usually smartly dressed, clean and tidy. I used to notice, in particular, his shoes—always well-brushed and of good quality.

McGuinness was not a man who would stand out in a crowd, nor would he want to. If anything, he was nondescript and incapable of making a lasting impression—except, that is, for the basilisk eyes.

No, he was not built like a Stallone or a Schwarzenegger, but, in his own way, he might be more than a match for them. He was to cause me many moments of chilling fear and, on one occasion, had me checking the upstairs windows of my home in the middle of the night—just in case. . . .

'Tank' got his nickname from his undoubted expertise in the specialised field of blowing safes, or 'tanks'. He was never a difficult client, never a know-all, and accepted my advice without argument when he was in trouble with the law. If I decided that the evidence was such that he should not waste the time of the court, he would dutifully allow me to plead guilty on his behalf. He was a realist and never insulted me by giving me statements in his defence which were palpably flawed.

I knew that he was a reasonable husband and father, and would do anything for his wife and family. Theirs was a strong family bond. He kept most of his criminal associates well away from his family and, if he were active, for example, in the field of house-breaking, he would stay away from his home for perhaps several days.

In the years before the Meehan case, I acted for 'Tank' in a variety of matters—from assault, theft and wilful fire-raising, to the more humdrum road traffic offences, such as driving while disqualified. I knew that he had a formidable reputation in the underworld and few people in Glasgow who knew him would care to cross him.

In August of 1972 he and another man were charged with the vicious murder of a man called Richards. It was a virtual assassination.

Frank Richards was a 35-year-old father of four who had been asleep in bed with his wife in their third storey flat in Sandaig Road, Barlanark. Under cover of the darkness of the early morning the killer, or killers, climbed the drainpipe and crept through an unlocked window. That morning, when the unfortunate Mrs Richards woke up at her usual time, she was horrified to find her husband lying dead beside her—stabbed through the heart.

One will understand now why I checked the windows of my own home during the night while I carried the secrets of 'Tank's' confessions!

Although arrested shortly after the Richards killing, the evidence against 'Tank' was, in my view, thin—a couple of unsuccessful identity parades, a plastercast of a footprint left on the window ledge, and an ambivalent statement made by him.

I was called in to represent the accused pair and saw them fairly frequently during the 90 days spent by them in the untried prisoners' wing of Barlinnie Prison. I wondered how the Crown could hope to bring them to trial with any hope of success, as both men vehemently denied the murder. I was not at all surprised when the Procurator Fiscal, Henry Herron, sent for me and told me that the Crown Office and the Lord Advocate had decided that the pair should be released at once.

In a situation like this—and there have been many—the prisoner is never told that the charge has been dropped, nor is his solicitor. He is simply released, without any comment from the prosecuting authorities. I suppose the reason for this apparently unsatisfactory state of affairs is that no one wishes to close the door to the possibility of new evidence coming to light in the future, which, perhaps, could considerably strengthen the hand of the Crown and so cause further action to be taken. Anyway, pleased with the news, I went to the prison so that I would be the first to advise my clients of the welcome tidings.

On their release half an hour later, they climbed into my car without speaking and I told them that it was extremely unlikely that we would hear any more about the matter. I counselled them to have no further discussion about the Richards murder with anyone.

I intended to give them a lift into town and I drove down Lee Avenue away from the prison and into Smithycroft Road. Within seconds of my turning McGuinness asked me to stop at the Anvil Bar. He invited me to join them in the bar for a celebratory drink. I turned down the invitation, as I always did. It is my invariable practice never to mix socially with clients. Despite the fact that 'Tank' had been a good source of business, I decided to make no exception to this golden rule of mine.

Some solicitors do mix with clients socially, perhaps not wishing to disappoint them, or to appear to be in any way stand-offish. Some solicitors pick up business in public houses, but I consider that to be on a par with the old-time 'ambulance chasers' whose activities were both embarrassing and infra dig in the pursuit of accident claims.

I stopped the car at the door of the Anvil and turned round to look at 'Tank'. He shrugged his shoulders at my rejecting his invitation. But, before opening the door to get out, he leaned forward across the back of my seat and, with his usual sullen expression—come to think of it, I don't think I ever saw him smile—quite unexpectedly, asked: 'You still interested in the Meehan case?'

I said, 'I always will be. Why do you ask?'

Now the Meehan case had never before been mentioned to me by 'Tank'. This was the first time he had even mentioned Meehan's name to me. Yes, I was extremely interested and waited anxiously to hear what he would say next. I didn't have to wait long.

'You defended an innocent man,' he stated, flatly.

Trying to engage him further, I said, 'How do you know, how can you be so certain?'

'I just know,' he drawled in his laconic way. He looked through me with those now familiarly penetrating eyes. 'I know,' he repeated.

Both he and his friend then left my car and I drove off slowly. I was deep in thought. Meehan's case had tortured me over the past three-and-a-half years, and here, out of the blue, was a member of the criminal world raising it unbidden.

'Tank' hadn't said much. He never did. But he had said enough. I thought, 'Why should he mention the Meehan case?' He would know of my deep involvement, perpetuated in the country's media, because I had made it clear that the case would not be allowed to rest with Meehan in prison for a murder he did not commit.

Why should 'Tank' give me this information within a quarter-of-an-hour of the triumph of his own release from prison? If this were a lifeline, I could not wait until I saw 'Tank' again. He hadn't said much but the intonation was significant—and the touch of menace. . . .

When he had said, 'I know', finally, there was a decided emphasis on the pronoun 'I'. I formed the view there and then that this had been quite intentional, and that he was clearly giving me time to mull the matter over.

This was the man who, over the next three years, was to say a lot more. It was destined to be a frustrating time in the future—a once-in-a-lifetime experience, which is more than enough for any man.

It was shortly after that when McGuinness began dropping in on me at my office. . . . For three years I was torn between the knowledge of the grim story that 'Tank' was to reveal in dribs and drabs, and the fact that such information was so strictly confidential.

This inviolable confidentiality I found hard to accept and take—after all, we were talking about a foul and dastardly murder for which Patrick Meehan, an innocent man, was serving a life sentence.

2

Eight days after Mrs Rachel Ross was found dying following the robbery at her home at 2 Blackburn Place, Ayr, Patrick Meehan was arrested and charged with her murder. He was also charged with assaulting her husband, Abraham, and with robbery of £1,800 and a number of traveller's cheques. Strongly suspected as his accomplice in the robbery and murder was his friend, James Griffiths.

A murder case, in which I was to become so involved, had begun. And with it came an extraordinary series of coincidences. These coincidences began on 5 July 1969, a Saturday afternoon—the day before the murder.

That day Meehan and Griffiths decided to go from Glasgow to Stranraer, down the Ayrshire coast, to 'case' or reconnoitre the Motor Taxation offices there, with a view to a future break-in. On the way to Stranraer—and on the way back—they passed through the town of Ayr. Neither Meehan or Griffiths were aware, as they set out on that journey, that two other men were planning a robbery in that same town that same night.

This was to be the first of two astonishing coincidences which would eventually prove too much for a few members of the jury at Meehan's eventual trial for murder.

The other coincidence was the evidence at that murder trial of the murdered woman's husband that he heard, in the course of a terrifying robbery, the two raiders refer to themselves as 'Pat' and 'Jim', the first names of Meehan and Griffiths.

My first connection with this celebrated case came on 14 July when my office in Glasgow's West George Street received a telephone call from Betty Meehan, asking that I go to Ayr police station and see Patrick Meehan who was being held there.

(Meehan has recently stated in a book written by him that I received my instructions to act for him from Detective Chief Superintendent Tom Goodall, then head of Glasgow CID. Indeed, he claims in his book—quite wrongly—that when I first met him at Ayr police station I told him this.

I do not receive instructions to act for people from police officers— the late Tom Goodall or anyone else!

Although I had never met Meehan at that time, one of my partners had acted earlier that same year for Betty Meehan in a divorce action against her husband, as he then had been. That being the case, there was nothing at all strange in her contacting my office—through my secretary Miss McBryan—when Meehan was arrested. Personally, my knowledge of my firm's acting for Betty came some time after his arrest. Being reasonably departmentalised at that time—the same applies today—I tried to take no part whatsoever in matters other than criminal.

Meehan, in his book, goes on to make assertions that I acted intentionally against his interests. I need hardly dignify these cruel remarks with an answer. I refute them in their hopelessly flawed entirety.

I received the message in the late afternoon, as I had been in court most of the day. After office hours I travelled to Ayr, where I met Meehan for the first time. I had had no prior personal dealings with the man. He was then 40 years old and had never in the past been charged with a crime of violence. But, of course, he had many convictions for dishonesty.

I was shown into a small ante-room at police headquarters, to find Meehan already there. He looked extremely angry.

I saw a stocky man, about five feet eight inches tall, with fair, reddish hair, close cut, with a side parting of sorts. He had a ruddy complexion and his face was unmarked. He looked to me to be of powerful build, weighing about ten stones. There was nothing remarkable about his dress, so far as I can recall.

I will never forget his opening remark to me, a stranger. 'If you think I did this hellish murder then I don't want you to act on my behalf. There are plenty of lawyers, after all.'

He stared at me and was obviously testing my reaction. I thought,

'What absolute cheek, what an introduction!' I told him I had an entirely open mind on the matter and knew next to nothing of the circumstances. I found him to be abrasive, but realised that he must be under a great deal of strain.

Somehow, even then, within the police station at Ayr, I came to sense that this was to be no ordinary case—and how right I was!

Meehan was a product of Glasgow's Gorbals. There was no real reason why he should have drifted into a life of crime, but he did, seeking to exist on thieving. He was to develop a certain skill in opening lockfast premises and safes. But he was not a successful criminal, living from theft to theft—and a good deal of that living was in prisons up and down the country.

It might be as well to mention here certain extraordinary claims that Meehan was to make about his earlier involvement with the Secret Services of Britain and East Germany! Meehan insisted that he had been approached in the sixties by a Communist agent and, after he had succeeded in one of his escapes from prison, had made his way to East Germany. His idea was to discuss with the KGB how they could effect the escape of certain spies who were at that time serving long sentences in British jails. One of these was George Blake, serving a sentence of 42 years for passing British naval secrets to the Russians.

Meehan claimed he ended up somewhere inside East Germany, being interrogated by the KGB, who later returned him to the West. He was met at the checkpoint by West German police, spirited to the British Consulate, flown to London and lodged in Wandsworth Prison, to finish the rest of his sentence.

While he was in prison, he said he warned MI5 that the Russians were interested in freeing Blake. He said that the British Secret Service did nothing about it—and, shortly afterwards, Blake was, indeed, freed from Wormwood Scrubs and spirited to the East.

At first I treated his claims and protestations that MI5 had framed him for the Ayr murder—in order 'to silence' him—with derision. I thought he was slightly paranoid about the whole matter, to say the least. But, looking back, there was something special about this case— an extremely strange case, with most unusual police reactions to myself and Meehan.

Yes, there was an extraordinary hostility towards us. I often wondered why. Clearly, this was not a normal murder charge—there was too much determination for a conviction, so much so that I found it difficult to cope with. Something made it a different 'ball game'—

and, with the benefit of hindsight, that could have stemmed from some kind of MI5 involvement.

As for Meehan, I was to find that he was a sharp and intelligent man, with a good memory, and quite well-read. But he was not a likeable person, particularly when matters were not going his way. He was inconsiderate of others and selfish. I was to find that he had a nasty streak in him.

But I believed him when he said that he had not committed the murder with which he was charged that day in Ayr police station. He told me of his movements on the night and morning of the murder— the trip to Stranraer and what he had done there, along with his accomplice and now vitally crucial alibi witness, Jim Griffiths, who, so far, had not been arrested. He was more than clear as to his total and complete innocence and I remembered him saying to me, 'I hate violence. I have no time for it. The bastards who did this should hang.'

I told him that I appreciated the value of Griffiths as a witness— two witnesses are usually better than one (particularly if the one happens to be the accused) and asked him how I could contact Griffiths right away. He asked me to call in on Betty Meehan on my way back. He said that she would know how to contact Irene Cameron, a girl who was befriending Griffiths. Through her, I would get to Griffiths.

Thus finished our very first meeting—how many hundreds I've had since!

I made tracks for the Meehan household at the high flats at Old Rutherglen Road, in the very heart of Glasgow's Gorbals.

My journey had started—one that would propel me into a maelstrom of thrilling events that would cover a period of 15 full and anxious years. It was a journey that would only end with the triumphant receipt of a cheque for substantial damages from St Andrew's House, Edinburgh, and the final expunction of any trace or suspicion of guilt.

I spoke to Betty Meehan with my request to find Griffiths. She fully understood the value of an early meeting and phoned Irene Cameron. Within minutes Irene appeared at the door. She was young, reasonably tall and attractive. She wore spectacles. I told her of my wish to meet her boyfriend and she replied that she would see to it that he would phone me at my Bothwell home later that night. I arranged to take statements from both of them next day.

Before leaving, I had phoned home and had spoken to my mother-in-law who lived with us. I told her that I would have a meal out and would be home after ten o'clock. I told her, too, that an Englishman might phone for me and, if so she should tell him to phone back at about 11 p.m. I stressed to my mother-in-law the importance of this contact. (Incidentally, my wife and family were on holiday in Minorca at this time. They normally spent July and August there in the villa we then had.)

I arrived home at about ten-thirty and was told that a man with an English accent had phoned earlier. My mother-in-law told me that he sounded extremely anxious, if not positively agitated. She had asked him to phone back that same evening.

I waited in vain for him to phone again. Had Griffiths done so, events might well have taken a dramatic turn—indeed, there might have been neither need nor reason to write this. Had he phoned back I would have arranged to meet him first thing in the morning, taken his full statement and then accompanied him to the Ayr police headquarters. Regrettably, although I waited up till after one o'clock in the morning, Griffiths did not phone back. I would never speak to, or meet, my 'star' alibi witness.

Next day, I travelled to Ayr Sheriff Court, arriving at 9.30 a.m. What a crowd had gathered—some 300 waited ominously in Wellington Square. It reminded me of a Wild West lynching mob. They were waiting for Meehan's arrival and it did not seem to be out of mere interest. One must remember that nine days had elapsed between the murder and this first appearance of Meehan and that the dreadful circumstances of the crime had never been out of TV and Press in the interim. The CID had been badgered by the media to make arrests— such was the considerable pressure on them.

We did not have long to wait. A large blue police van arrived abruptly at the main entrance. The rear door opened, two uniformed police officers emerged, followed by two CID officers and the stocky figure of a man with a coat hiding his face and shoulders. The man was guided from the van by the CID officers and was taken up the six steps.

The crowd began to roar and shout, as if out of control. 'Bastard', 'Cunt', 'Hang him', 'Fucking murderer', could be heard above the rabble. Some surged forward for an ugly moment and at least one young man kicked Meehan, although at that stage he did not even know his name or who he was. The assailant knew nothing of the case against the prisoner, had clearly forgotten the law's proud boast of an accused being innocent until proved guilty, and he assumed, as they all did that eventful, never-to-be-forgotten morning, that the police had arrested the man responsible for the crime. The thought of a trial had escaped them as they shouted for Meehan's blood.

I was just behind my client on the steps and pushed some of the throng to one side. The police officers, in their understandable haste, half-carried him into the temporary safety of the court building. We rushed upstairs and then to a small, austere room next to Ayr's Court Number One.

By this time Meehan's face was no longer concealed and his hair was dishevelled. His eyes were popping out of his head. He turned to one of the CID officers—a tall and heavily built man—grabbed him by his coat lapels and shouted at him, 'Do your fucking job, go to Stranraer and check my alibi. I know nothing about this bloody murder. Get the bastards who did it.'

I moved in fast and pulled him away, telling him to keep his cool and that all aspects of his defence would be thoroughly investigated by the police, and by myself. By the time of the trial three months later the officer who was virtually assaulted by Meehan in this room completely forgot about the incident and told the court that he had no recollection whatsoever of being pulled and pushed and, indeed, threatened by Meehan.

We were then left alone in the room, no doubt with several officers on the other side of the unlocked door. Meehan looked frighteningly furious and spoke about the injustice he had just experienced at the very entrance to the court. He seemed to despair.

This state was exacerbated when I told him of Griffiths' inability to make contact with me. 'He's panicked when he heard of my arrest.'

It is worth knowing that Meehan in his befuddled and confused state clearly thought that he would have been released following the supporting testimony of alibi of his friend Griffiths. He was wrong, of course—both would then have been charged with the Ayr murder. Meehan told me: 'You'll need to get him. I need him to clear me.'

His first of many court appearances took place about an hour later, when I escorted him before Sheriff George Reid for the formal hearing. Even this was unusual because after being identified in the sheriff's private chambers—at this early stage of a serious case neither public nor Press are allowed into the court as it is held *in camera*—he decided on the unusual course, and on my advice, to 'emit a Declaration'.

Normally these proceedings would last all of 30 seconds, when the solicitor would merely say, 'No plea, no Declaration.' To the surprise of the court officials, this emission of a Declaration by the accused sent the clerk scurrying off to look for the printed forms used on such rare occasions.

After the inevitable delay the statement of my client was noted formally by the sheriff in the following terms: 'I know absolutely nothing about this murder. Griffiths and I went to Stranraer, I agree, but neither of us set foot in Ayr.'

Many a sheriff and fiscal go through their 30 years of service without experiencing such procedure, so seldom does an accused wish to commit himself at this embryonic stage of proceedings.

Later that same day, matters went through the roof. . . .

3

Unknown to me, in his sheer desperation, Meehan had given the police the Glasgow address of Griffiths at 14 Holyrood Crescent. He wanted him to be interviewed—for patently obvious reasons.

That same afternoon I was to learn of the next dramatic phase in the hunt for the murderers of Mrs Ross—the shoot-out at Holyrood Crescent. Details were on the television news and in the later editions of the Glasgow *Evening Times*.

I phoned Detective Chief Superintendent Tom Goodall—head of Glasgow CID, who was very well-known to me—to find out what had happened. I had found him obliging in the past and quite helpful. Indeed, later on, I was to seek him out at an advanced stage of my preparation for the Meehan trial. Sheer worry caused me to contact Goodall. I was given much more detail by him on the phone, my heart sinking with each piece of news.

Briefly, what happened was that the police, having been given his address by Meehan, hastily obtained a warrant for the arrest of Griffiths. Two detectives then called and interviewed the flat's caretaker. No attempt was made at this stage to speak to Griffiths and they left shortly afterwards.

It was so unfortunate and catastrophic that Meehan had not told me that same morning of his having divulged this now famous address. At ten-thirty in the morning a number of CID officers, including members of the Scottish Regional Crime Squad, arrived at No. 14 and stealthily ascended the stairs to the top flat. They knocked loudly on the door, time and again, shouting who they were—that they were police officers and that they wanted to speak to James Griffiths.

Eventually, one of the officers kicked the door in—to be met with a fusillade of shots as Griffiths came at them with a shotgun. Bandoliers of ammunition were strapped round his body.

What a shock this must have been to the five officers! They descended with speed, assisting their colleague, Detective Constable William Walker, who had been hit. After all, they were unarmed.

Griffiths came after them and, from the upper landing, fired again at the retreating figures. As they arrived in the street they heard bursts of gunfire coming from the top flat window. This was clearly indiscriminate shooting and one could excuse pedestrians and police alike running for cover. Armed with a shotgun and a telescopic rifle, Griffiths was firing at everything and anyone who moved. A pedestrian, a man merely minding his own business, was shot in the leg. Within seconds another innocent passer-by was badly wounded.

The gunman seemed to have a deathwish—such was his determination not to surrender to the police. Who knows, had he been in any way responsible for the Ayr murder he might have given up without such ado, but I know he was innocent and, perhaps, for all I know, this was the very first time he was being sought after by police officers for a major crime *not* perpetrated by him. Such might have been the irony of the action-packed situation.

The windows of nearby houses received no immunity from the hail of bullets. The unfortunate police officers radioed for assistance and, within minutes, most Glasgow units knew of the grim affray and headed for the spot with all speed.

Detective Chief Superintendent Tom Goodall arrived and took immediate command. Weapons had been issued to many officers on his instructions and the area around Holyrood Crescent was sealed off.

At the same time, the gunman left Holyrood Crescent and was seen to remove more cartridges from the boot of a car parked there. He then re-entered No. 14. Four more members of the police were to fall wounded, closely followed by a fifth.

The operation was escalating by the second and several police marksmen arrived. The area was by now like a battlefield. Men were lying injured, with teams of ambulancemen trying to get to them. Tracker dogs and their handlers littered the area.

As suddenly as it started, the shooting stopped. People wondered why. Griffiths, in fact, had disappeared, having entered the back garden, climbed the high wall and reached Lansdowne Crescent Lane, without being spotted. He made his way into North Woodside Road and re-started his shooting—this time at a number of pedestrians, who fled in terror.

As he reached Henderson Street, with the police by this time in close pursuit, he saw an unfortunate Jim Kerr enter his firm's car. He bounded towards him and fired through the space caused by the wound-down driver's window. The driver was struck on his left arm and collapsed out of the car, screaming in pain. Griffiths jumped into the car and drove off.

By that time army reinforcements had arrived, as well as teams of Pressmen and TV reporters. A vigilant member of the public told marksman Chief Superintendent Malcolm Finlayson of the direction the hijacked car had taken.

Suddenly, a car emerged from nearby Garriochmill Road—like a bat out of hell, such was its speed. It turned sharply into North Woodside Road. The driver was recognised and the car number relayed to all police cars in the neighbourhood, and there were many.

Griffiths crashed the car near the Round Toll—this was not surprising, from the speed and the erratic, panic-stricken driving. He rushed into the Round Toll Bar in Possil Road, still brandishing his firearms and bearing his bandoliers. He shut the door behind him and, like any Wild West gunslinger, glared at the manager and his numerous happy-go-lucky customers, all enjoying a quiet drink. He shattered the tranquillity by shouting, 'I'll shoot anyone who moves. I've already shot four policemen.'

In Doc Holliday fashion, he then fired two shots in the high ceiling. A third shot struck poor William Hughes in the chest and caused him to hit the floor. He later died from this wound. The unfortunate Hughes had, in fact, moved only to put down his very last pint measure.

Brazenly, Griffiths then demanded a drink—as if anyone could refuse such a request. He was handed a bottle of brandy and coolly started drinking from its neck.

While this drama was unfolding the police were moving in.

Then John Connelly, the pub's chargehand, with complete disregard for his own safety, suddenly advanced on the deranged gunman and pushed him outside the bar premises. It was possibly an impetuous action, done without due thought and consideration for himself and his own safety. Griffiths reappeared within seconds and fired three shots at the brave Mr Connelly. The shots were wild and no further injury was caused.

The sound of gunfire attracted many people to the scene, among them Mr John Craig, a lorry driver. In the meantime local hero John Connelly was pursuing his assailant who had fled from his public house. Craig stopped his lorry close to the bar—no doubt wondering what the hell was going on—when Griffiths, still carrying both guns, approached him. Wisely, Craig left his vehicle and took shelter nearby. He watched helplessly as Griffiths entered his lorry and drove off northwards in Possil Road. Two other men were wounded at this stage, each one falling to the pavement in obvious pain. Poor Craig must have been perplexed and looked around for the possible film crews.

Griffiths drove at speed to Keppochhill Road, past Sighthill Cemetery and into Springburn Road, and then made a sharp screeching left turn into Kay Street. Finlayson and other officers were not far behind in a police Landrover. Other police cars were alerted and began closing in on the fleeing gunman.

Meanwhile, Griffiths saw that he had entered a cul-de-sac, because Kay Street was well and truly that. Not to be outdone, he jumped from the lorry and ran up the stairs of the last tenement building. It was a small, two-storey building rapidly reaching a dilapidated state. He forced his way into the house on the upper landing, possibly not realising that no one had seen where he had gone.

His luck was in, the house was empty and one could only speculate as to what would have happened had he decided to lie low and wait patiently. This was not to be. Shots were soon heard from the top flat window at 26 Kay Street. He had betrayed his own hideout. Had he a deathwish?

Rapidly he moved to the rear of the house and began random firing in the direction of a children's playground in Elmvale Street. The playground was packed with children and their unsuspecting parents. This did not deter the irrational gunman. There was a further salvo of shots which caused 18-year-old Mrs Reid and eight-year-old Peter Traynor to collapse with flesh wounds. Another pedestrian was wounded outside the front of the house.

The flat was by now entirely cordoned off, with police in ever-increasing attendance. Finlayson and Detective Sergeant Ian Smith, who was also armed, made their hazardous way to the close mouth at No. 26. Both had .38 revolvers at the ready. They raced up the stairs

to the damaged door and found the upstairs landing strewn with
spent cartridge cases.

Finlayson looked through the letterbox and peered inside. He saw
that the lobby floor was also littered with spent cartridge cases. He
heard the sound of more shooting and then Griffiths appeared in his
sights as he ran into the narrow lobby—still very much armed and
reminiscent of a modern-day Rambo-type apparition. He saw Finlayson's eyes and made for him.

'It was either Griffiths or myself,' he was later to say. 'I took my .38
and aimed it through the letterbox and fired at his shoulder.'

I don't think I would have been so choosy in such a matter for sur-
vival.

Griffiths collapsed on his knees but, as he was falling, still managed
to fire towards the door. Bursting into the flat, both officers fell upon
him and disarmed him. Seconds later Griffiths died in a pool of his
own blood. Finlayson's bullet had missed the shoulder and entered his
chest.

Full marks for the courage shown by both officers, who were later
to be decorated for the bravery of their actions, which were in the
very best traditions of the Glasgow Force. But the crazed, desperate
gunman was dead—his alibi testimony would never be heard.

In a period of time telescoped into 90 minutes Griffiths had killed a
man, wounded five detective officers and injured 11 civilians. What a
toll—indeed, even the Glasgow of *No Mean City* fame had never seen
its like. Some civilians were also decorated for the part they had
played in one of the City's worst hours.

By late afternoon I was aware of most of the foregoing details and
remember sagging in my office seat and saying to myself, 'What
next?' After dinner, however, I rushed to the prison and, on the way, I
remember thinking—if Griffiths were innocent, as Meehan so surely
states, then why on earth should he virtually commit suicide? Because
that is, in effect, what he clearly did. I was anxious to gauge Meehan's
reaction to my news and to put my earlier thought-out question to
him. Surely, I thought, any future jury would assess Griffiths' actions
in a way adverse to Meehan's interests. And could one blame them?

As I reached the prison's environs I knew that matters were
desperate and, probably for the first and only time in my dealings
with him, I carried the gravest of doubts in my head as to his innocence.

Unfortunately, neither Meehan nor I knew anything at all, at that time, of an earlier programme by BBC television, based on Griffiths, just before he was so recently released from Gartree Prison. The content was so important that I obtained the tape from the BBC shortly after I heard about it. Regrettably, this was in the period between Meehan's conviction and his appeal.

The value of the tape was twofold. The main drift of a recorded interview with Griffiths—then on the verge of freedom—was that he would never be back in prison . . . he had had enough. On being asked if that meant that he would be going 'straight' on his release, he replied, strangely, 'No, not at all, I am too fond of the good things in life—but they'll never get me next time.'

'They', I would think, would be the authorities, through the police.

'They'll never lock me up again,' he volunteered. This rash statement, laced with bravado, put an entirely different complexion on the fracas at Holyrood Crescent.

Griffiths, never a stupid man, must have realised that Meehan would soon give his address to the police in his dire desperation. After all, Griffiths failed to make contact with me despite his promise to my mother-in-law.

Nevertheless, there he was, alone and heavily armed in his attic flat, as if in anticipation of the fireworks yet to come. Clearly he had decided to honour his Gartree statements and ensure that he would never again be taken alive.

If I'm wrong about this then why didn't Griffiths drive off into oblivion on the night of the 14th, in the car that we know he had parked near to his flat? He would have a start of some 24 hours and was barely known in Scotland. Why did he wait for the inevitable, in his makeshift armoury?

It must be considered, too, that, in all probability, Meehan would not have divulged his address to the police had he known of the presence of firearms and ammunition there. This would have been a dreadful preamble to the alibi evidence he knew that only Griffiths could supply on his behalf.

One must also be reminded of the fact that Griffiths was already 'wanted' in England on several theft warrants, and, as I have already said, he was in possession of a stolen car, together with an array of weapons and ammunition. For these matters alone he would have gone down for a very substantial period of time, particularly with his appalling criminal record. Add to that the possibility—nay, certainty—of being charged with the dreadful Ayr murder, along with an equally innocent man.

4

I booked myself in at the prison, where I found that Meehan was unaware of the afternoon's happenings and was quite shocked when I told him about them.

'I don't understand it,' he said 'How can that be?' He was clearly shaken and realised, to the full, the obvious implications.

I said, 'Doing what he did would indicate to me that he had something to fear if he came forward—perhaps that he was responsible for the murder.'

Meehan resented what I said and maintained the complete innocence of himself and Griffiths—and reminded me of what he had said on the previous day within the Ayr cells: 'If you're in doubt about me, then don't act.'

I must say that I was impressed by his reaction to this extraordinary situation.

'I don't know why he did it but he was as innocent as I am,' he repeated. 'I know it looks bad but they can't convict an innocent man, can they?'

I finished by telling him that I was going back to see his wife and Irene Cameron in order to take statements. When I left him there was a marked resurgence in my confidence.

Next morning, however, I was dumped again—up and down I was, like a jack-in-the-box. Every national morning newspaper in Scotland carried details of the Holyrood Crescent shoot-out—well, that was understandable and to be expected. In addition, however, and with equal prominence, was a Crown Office hand-out by our Crown agent, Stan Bowen. Every morning paper had it, as had BBC-TV and STV, as well as the evenings. I was outraged as I read the papers at home. My heart sank and not without good reason. I was accustomed to reasonably fair play from the Crown in my earlier 13 years' experience at this level—not body-blows, and below the belt at that. . . .

The statement was brief and terse. It was as follows: 'With the death of Griffiths and the apprehension of Patrick Meehan, the police are no longer looking for any other person suspected of implication in the incident concerning Mr and Mrs Ross at Ayr.'

This type of statement had no precedent—it had not happened before, nor, thankfully, has it occurred since. I wondered and agonised as to why it should have been made. Could the reason have been that the Crown, at this very earliest of stages, wished to support the actions of the police at the siege of Holyrood Crescent and publicly exonerate them from the shooting of Griffiths?

I don't know, but I conferred again with my client and sent at once my reply to the Crown Office. I saw to it that the Press of the land knew what I was doing. I was not accepting this without protest.

My fear was that this outlandish statement, from what purports to be a responsible body, would poison the minds of future jurors who might be called to sit in judgment on my client in some three months' time. Surely, I thought, the Crown would never stoop to this level? Then why make such a statement at all? It was now only 16 July and I kept asking myself at that very early stage, 'What's so special about this case? There's something odd here.'

I then wrote a letter to try to undo some of the damage already done by this statement—misleadingly inviting in its appearance and grossly unfair in its content. Meehan demanded immediate action on this most recent outrage and this I gave him.

I wrote in the following terms to the Crown Agent:

It would now be near impossible for my client to have a fair trial before an unbiased jury. The Crown Office statement with regard to the finality of the police enquiries perturbs me.

This would appear to mean that the police are satisfied that they can exclude any possibility of error or mistake. In my opinion, in the particular circumstances of this case, there might well be a possibility of a mistake. I am far from satisfied that this possibility can be excluded. My client is entitled to a presumption of innocence.

Following the Crown Office statement it might well appear to some that he is now required to prove his innocence, whereas Scots Law demands that the prosecution must prove his guilt. I therefore feel that my client's case has been irreparably prejudiced.

Hard on the heels of receiving a fairly anaemic reply, the authorities now compounded the prejudice—because that there clearly was—by two further reprehensible actions.

They 'leaked' to the Press the complete criminal record of Griffiths. It should be observed that had Griffiths been wounded and not killed—in other words had he survived to stand trial—his record could not and would not be published, for clear and obvious reasons.

Secondly, as if the foregoing were not enough, they inserted in the *Police Gazette* an announcement that it was now known (not 'thought' or 'believed' to be the case) that the car that had taken part in the Ayr robbery and murder was a blue Triumph 2000, registration number and all.

In addition to complaining about the unfairness of the Crown Office statement, Meehan now also told me about an identification parade that had taken place at the CID Headquarters in Turnbull Street, Glasgow, several hours before he had seen me for the first time. He wasn't over-pleased about that either. . . .

A solicitor called Peter T. McCann had represented him at this parade. (McCann later became the Lord Provost of Glasgow.) Meehan's complaint—a valid one, I thought—was that at no time prior to the parade was he told that it was the intention of the Crown to have not only the normal visual identification, but that he would be asked to speak, too. McCann could not continue to act in this manner because he was friendly with a close relation of Abraham Ross. After seeing Meehan for the very first time at Ayr Police H.Q. I telephoned McCann that evening, as a matter of courtesy, who confirmed the situation, stating that he had no further interest in the case.

He was immensely confident at the parade—and that's why he took up position number one. Had he had prior knowledge of the voice request it is more likely that he would have 'buried' himself in its middle.

I have attended certain parades where the line-up was asked to speak, but I had always been advised of this unusual aspect in advance of the parade. The situation at present has been revised—perhaps as a result of this particular parade.

At any rate, he took up position number one, confident that he would be cleared.

Although neither Meehan nor Griffiths had set foot in Ayr at the time of the robbery at the Ross home, Meehan, I now learned, had told the police [initially by phone] that he and Griffiths had seen an incident at a lay-by outside Kilmarnock. It seemed that when he read the numerous Press reports about the murder, he, at the insistence of his wife and daughter, had phoned the police and given them details of the happening.

Griffiths had been driving the Triumph 2000 some distance out of Ayr on the homeward journey and near Kilmarnock in the small hours, when Meehan noticed a teenage girl on the road ahead, clearly distraught. He asked Griffiths to stop, which he did. The car was then reversed to where the girl was standing. Meehan had asked her what had happened and was told that she and her girlfriend had been given a lift from Prestwick from two boys in an old, light-coloured car. One of the boys tried to 'get funny' with her in the back of the car. She had objected—as a result of which she had been put out of the car at the lay-by. The car had driven off minutes earlier, with her friend still in it.

Meehan told her to get into the back of the Triumph and asked Griffiths to drive off in pursuit. A mile or so on they overtook a white car and Meehan signalled the driver to pull up by waving his hand outside the nearside front window. The car duly stopped and Meehan told his girl passenger to tell her pal to leave the other car, which she did. After that, they drove both girls to an address in Kilmarnock—and 'mighty relieved' they were.

In general conversation Meehan remembered that one of the girls was named Burns, causing him to make some remark about Scotland's most famous bard.

Days before his arrest Meehan had told the police about this incident on the phone—although anonymously. He thought the two male occupants of the other car just might know something about the murder that occupied most of the headlines.

Thus the two Kilmarnock girls were brought to view the parade— Irene Burns and Isobel Smith. They were obviously nervous and Meehan said to each of them, clearly identifying himself in the process: 'It's all right, pet, don't worry about it.' Understandably, they picked him out.

Other witnesses who had seen something at the murder scene—Mr Falconer, Mrs Mathieson and Mr Haxton—picked out no one.

Finally, the crunch came. Abraham Ross was assisted into the parade room, clearly under drugs and ill-at-ease, and taken to the far end of the parade—that is, to position number one (Meehan). The officer in charge of the parade then asked Meehan to say the following: 'Shut up, shut up, we'll send for an ambulance.' Meehan was the first to be asked to repeat these words.

This was probably, indeed, I am certain, the first time that Ross had heard these words spoken to him since his dreadful experience at his home. He was under sedation—his hospital nurse was with him—and one can readily anticipate what his reaction would be, irrespective of who repeated the nightmarish nine words that were so clearly and indelibly imprinted in his memory.

The reaction of Abraham Ross was understandable, I think.

Ashen-faced, he almost collapsed. He cried, 'That's the voice, I know it, I know it! I don't have to go any further.'

Meehan retorted at once, 'You're mistaken, laddie.' He went on to say, 'Sir, you've got the wrong man, honest.'

The parade broke up at that. No other stand-in (and there were five) was asked to repeat the ghastly words. That was it. Meehan was then charged by the officer in control of the case, Superintendent Struthers. His reply was in keeping, 'You are making a horrible mistake. I know absolutely nothing about it'.

It is unfortunate that Ross only heard one voice. Had Meehan 'buried' himself within the line-up, as most do, one must wonder what the reaction of Ross would have been to hearing numbers one, two, three, four or five speaking. We shall never know, but the suspect should have known in advance the full significance of the parade and all that it entailed. Equally, his solicitor ought to have been alerted.

Questions were asked later of the conduct of the parade, when it was established conclusively that Ross viewed the parade last and not first as he, the official parade record and other officers erroneously stated.

Hindsight is always helpful, but had I been present at the parade and realised that voice was of the essence then even at that late stage, towards the end of the parade, I would have stopped it there and then, as I have done in the past. I would have asked Ross to retire from the room and then would have ensured that the first speaker would not be the suspect. In other words I would have altered the line-up, with Meehan possibly in position three or four.

Meehan also told me about a statement he had made to the police on 12 July at his home, without making any request for a solicitor to be present. The statement read:

About 4 p.m. on Saturday 5th July, along with an English friend of mine called Jim Griffiths, we left Glasgow in Jim's car, a blue Triumph

2000, which he had a loan of from a friend in England to go to Stranraer to see a motor car which was for sale in a garage near Stranraer police station.

After we left Glasgow I don't know the road we took but we arrived in Stranraer about seven o'clock. Griffiths was driving. When we arrived there we went to the garage and we spoke to an old man who was in charge of the petrol pumps.

He could not tell us anything about the car we were interested in so we left the garage.

I then went with Griffiths to a tea room where we had high tea. We stayed in the tea room for about an hour and a half. After we left the tearoom Jim said he was going to the car to fix the indicator handle which had broken. He said it would take a while and he had to remove a part of the dashboard. I told him I would just go for a walk around the town.

I walked down to the harbour where I had a drink in a pub. I left the pub and stood watching the car ferry being loaded. After that I went to a different pub where I stayed till closing time.

After I left the pub I walked about for a while. As I was passing the station a girl spoke to me and asked if I knew the time of the bus to a local village. I can't remember its name. I spoke to someone—or it could have been a driver—and asked the time of the bus and then told the girl.

I walked back to where Jim was sorting the indicator. When I got there he told me he hadn't managed to fix it. A while later—I think it would be midnight—both of us left to go back to Glasgow. I don't know the way we came back, but I remember seeing the Airport at Prestwick.

He then went on to describe the happenings at the lay-by near Kilmarnock.

We then drove back to Glasgow, getting there, I think, about 5 a.m. When I got up on the Sunday I phoned Stranraer police to get the name of the garage where I was making enquiries the day before about a Morris 1100. I then, I think, on either Tuesday or Wednesday this week, saw in the papers that a woman had been murdered in Ayr at the weekend. I then told my wife about the girls we'd given a lift on the Sunday morning. She told me I'd better report it to the police. I didn't want to report it as I didn't like getting involved with the police. My daughter said I would be better to report it.

On Wednesday I telephoned the police at Ayr and told them about the girls we had picked up. When I phoned I could not remember the girls' names. I did not say who I was when I phoned. A short time later

I remembered one of the girl's names as being Burns. I then phoned the police again at Ayr and told them the girl's name. I did not give them my name.

This was an extremely detailed and lengthy statement which could easily be confirmed in its aspects—and was. Seldom are initial statements as long as this. It was as if Meehan was inviting the police to confirm every detail. The Crown position at the trial in respect of the Burns lay-by incident was that they accepted it—indeed, they could hardly do anything else—but argued that this had happened *after* the robbery and murder.

In short, if Meehan and Griffiths had been those responsible and were in the process of making their getaway, they took time off from this task to assist two young girls, unknown to them, in distress. They invited both into the 'getaway' car and ran the risk of them seeing their loot, not to mention giving them every chance to identify each of them! That such a professional job should be committed by such amateurs is surely hard to imagine.

Next, I arranged for my brother, Raymond, a professional photographer with the Glasgow *Evening Times*, to accompany me to the prison, where several good 'close-ups' of Meehan were taken. I required these 'close-up' photographs in order to assist in establishing his alibi and having him identified in Stranraer.

5

I went with some of my staff to Stranraer and checked out Meehan's alibi.

The old man in the garage and a waitress in the tearoom recognised Meehan's photograph. Indeed, we managed to trace a man from one of the pubs who also recognised him. Matters were truly promising at that end. I was pleased to report these better tidings to Meehan. I suggested that in view of the shoot-out it might be better to cut himself away from Griffiths, but he would hear none of that.

'I stand by Griffiths,' he said. 'We're both innocent.'

Hard on the heels of the reply from Crown Office—they were not at all impressed by my letter of protest and the publicity it had received—I decided that we might have to go further than normal in this case: namely, try to prove his entire innocence, as opposed to sitting back and arguing, as then seemed to be the case, that the Crown could not prove guilt beyond reasonable doubt.

What, after all, had they got?—a dicey voice identification, his travelling through Ayr on his own admission around the same time, give or take a few hours, and Ross saying that the robbers addressed each other by the names 'Pat' and 'Jim'.

And this is where we come to the second extraordinary coincidence in this strange murder case.

One could well argue that only professionals would attempt such a 'tie-up' job, as it is called (particularly when conversation is liable to be required) and that they would be unlikely to use their own names and would arrange the necessary aliases in advance. Is it not the case that, in this neck of the woods, 'Pat' and 'Jim' are very very common Christian names and, as such, likely to be assumed or used? Despite what I considered to be a far-from-strong prosecution case, I felt we should try a step never taken before.

I took with me that day's newspaper, the headlines of which related to a young American film starlet called Sharon Tait who had been brutally murdered in her Californian home. She had been the wife of the famous Hollywood film producer, Roman Polanski. The article went on to say—and this is what grabbed my attention—that a house boy and suspect had been cleared of all involvement after he elected to be questioned by the police under a truth drug.

I knew little of the 'truth drug' at this time, but felt in a somewhat desperate situation following the unique and, hopefully never-to-be-repeated, Crown Office statement. As I drove to the prison I was also anxious to find out how Meehan would react to the novel situation I was about to confront him with.

I showed Meehan the newspaper with the house boy information underlined. I asked him how he would feel about an experiment—never done before—whereby he would be questioned by the police, in my presence, of course, after having been injected with the truth drug, or sodium pentothal with Methedrine, as it is medically known.

Any answer given by him in his drugged, semi-conscious state would be recorded on the spot and would be available as evidence at his trial. Even if the replies turned out to be adverse, in fairness, he would have to agree to their availability in court. The tape would be a production at his trial. He might be asked, for example, questions of the layout of the Ross bungalow, and other intimate details, known only to the assailant.

I asked him what he thought—and bear in mind he had no prior warning of my unusual offer—or, should I say, gamble? He replied, quick as a flash, 'Can you arrange for this to be done tonight?'

His spontaneous reaction merely reinforced my own certainty as to his innocence. I thought, 'If only the Crown Office officials could have been present at this meeting.' There was no trace of hesitation in his reply, no question of weighing up the pros and cons.

With much on my mind, I left him. So much had happened so far, yet he had been in custody for less than a week. In Scotland, unlike England, incidentally, a prisoner on any charge can only be detained without bail for a maximum period of 110 days. This provision puts a certain strain on the Crown, who must move reasonably fast—but this is a much healthier situation than that of an untried prisoner languishing indefinitely, sometimes for 18 months and longer, having no idea as to when his sojourn in jail will end. There had even been occasions abroad when accused persons would be tempted to sign confessions (truthful or otherwise) in order to bring a finality to their proceedings. Other countries, including England, should follow our lead, in my opinion.

Less than a week of the case ... and yet exceptional points were continuing to occur. I began to wonder if the Crown had something up their sleeve, a surprise for both Meehan and myself.

They had, although even the Crown were not aware of certain paper evidence at this stage. It was still under wraps.

Solicitors for accused persons are required to wait until the indictment is served before they can complete their enquiries into the Crown case. One usually receives this all-important document about one month before the commencement of the trial. In it, we find the final terms of the charge or charges, the list of prosecution witnesses (with addresses) to be called by the Crown, and a list of all documentary (written productions), as well as all label ones—that is, knife, cash, masks or other items to be used by the prosecution in support of its case. In sheriff and jury matters an indictment is signed by a Procurator Fiscal on behalf of the Lord Advocate, but in High Court affairs it is signed by an Advocate Depute, on behalf of the Lord Advocate.

I longed for a sight of this document, but I knew, or thought, that I would not receive it until the last day the law allows for its service on the accused. I was not disappointed, and was not to have it in my grasp for several anxious months to come.

When I arrived home in the evening of the day when I first mooted the truth drug to Meehan I called on my next door neighbour, Doctor J. Anthony Grogan, my own doctor at that time, a personal friend, and a police casualty surgeon employed in this part-time capacity by the Hamilton police department.

I was excited and showed him the newspaper article about Sharon Tait. I asked him what he knew of the truth drug. He gave me his views off the top of his head, but promised me that he would research the matter forthwith. I told him of the plan that was still forming in my head—what an effect on any future jury this experiment would have. Even news of this (which would have to be done pre-trial) would assist us—and I would see to it that the public at large would know all about it.

Some might think that these tactics were unfair to the Crown—but what of their infamous statement, and their proposed use of the Holyrood Crescent incident, both of which were hardly favourable to my now exasperated client? There was also the excitement of breaking new legal territory in Scotland. Even now I receive telephone calls from English solicitors requesting full details of my attempt to introduce such interrogation, whilst under a drug, into the law of Scotland.

I found it difficult to sleep that night. Indeed, I was to pester and badger my doctor friend for the next few days in my desire to find out as much I could about this new and promising field.

There were other points of significance with which I wrestled in bed—because they seemed to belie the arrogant optimism portrayed by the Crown in this never-to-be-forgotten public hand-out—particularly the fact that there was a complete absence of forensic evidence linking Meehan, or Griffiths, for that matter, to the Ross bungalow. Not a button, fibre, blood stain, hair or thread left by the two men the Crown claimed had ransacked the bungalow. Not a fingerprint—nothing.

There was also the fact that although Meehan and his home were thoroughly searched by the police, nothing of significance was found. Although this type of evidence is negative, it can be extremely telling. You can understand that in a full-scale enquiry, such as this was, the Ayr house would have been searched with a fine toothcomb for any trace of a clue leading to the culprits.

Another thought flashed through my now weary head. It was that due to the conduct of the honest men of Ayr outside the Court—and the bonnie lassies, too—it would be absolutely necessary to do my *utmost* to have the trial transferred from Ayr. There seemed to be just too much prejudice there, particularly when prospective jurors would be chosen from the area of the court where the trial would take place.

6

Next day Tony Grogan phoned me with news of the 'truth drug'. He had been good enough to telephone Canadian medical experts on the subject, and he, too, was brimming with excitement—and expectation.

Tony was a small, portly man with a very friendly disposition. A first-class doctor, he and I were educated at the same school and university, although he was several years younger than I. Tony had helped me on a number of occasions in the past with his medical expertise, but this was the first time I was about to ask him to be a witness for the defence. He frequently gave evidence for the Crown in Hamilton court cases.

He filled me in with the 'niceties' of the 'truth drug'—and told me it was by no means 100 per cent reliable. The basic idea behind the experiment was that the patient is drugged and remains only semi-conscious. That being the case, he is less inclined to be able to persist with a tissue of lies. He would also divulge points in answers to questions which could have a bearing on his credibility.

An example would be to ask him to describe the interior of the Ross bungalow (where he claimed he had never been) and to record his answers. He could also be asked questions based on the detailed precognition of Ross—such as what conversation had taken place within the bungalow. If intimate knowledge, known only to those responsible, were revealed, then this would be highly relevant and such special information would clearly count very much against him.

On the other hand, if it were clear that he hadn't a clue and that his

answers showed lack of knowledge, then surely one would be entitled
to draw a favourable inference.

The drug—sodium pentothal with Methedrine—would require to
be injected intravenously. There would also have to be an anaesthetist
present. There would be a recording machine, taping every question
and every answer.

I had decided that I would ask the questions, but that I would invite
the Procurator Fiscal of Ayr, and several CID top brass, to attend.
There was one obstacle. We would require to have this unique experiment take place in Barlinnie and I would need to write to the Governor there for his permission to allow the retinue of doctor, anaesthetist,
lawyer, Fiscal, police, recording technician and stenographer into his
prison. This I did. I also wrote to the Fiscal of Ayr and the local CID
chief and advised them of the parameters of my challenge.

Within days the Governor replied, telling me that he had conferred
with Crown Office and that he was refusing me permission for the
experiment within his premises.

I arranged an immediate consultation with Nicholas Fairbairn,
who had been selected by me to represent my client. We decided to
prepare a petition to the *Nobile Officium* of the High Court. Such
applications relate to unusual requests—as this certainly was—to the
court which has overriding power to make, if necessary, new procedure
or law. This court consists of three senior judges.

The *raison d'être* of our request, we said, was to ordain the Governor
to allow the persons, earlier referred to, access to Meehan at the
prison. Certainly, there was to be nothing of a clandestine or secret
nature in what we proposed to do.

We had every intention of proceeding with this dangerous matter,
were we to be given the go-ahead by the court. I say that because I
have no doubt that the powers that be, in particular some of the
senior judges of the High Court, formed the view that our actions
were 'gimmicky'. In other words, they thought that we were relying
on *not* being given permission, but using the whole matter to score
tactical points over the Crown and so boost Meehan's chances of
acquittal. One statement made by Lord Cameron at the subsequent
hearing, when our petition was dismissed, so persuades me. Towards
the conclusion of the proceedings he leaned forward, with his eyes
fixed on me, and said, 'It is the duty of this court to protect every
accused person from and against the folly of his legal adviser.' No
more required to be said. I was furious. Clearly, the reasons behind the

experiment had been misunderstood by those at the top. I was not in the business of scoring cheap points, but could not put this across to them.

The 'truth drug' application was heard and dismissed long before the commencement of the trial.

Before the hearing I had asked Tony to go to London and meet Dr Sargant there. This man had administered the compound in order to eliminate suspects from the famous case of the 'Boston Strangler'. He was the acknowledged expert in this field in the United Kingdom. When I phoned him after Tony's searching meeting with him he agreed to lead the experiment at Barlinnie prison—and without fee, such was his intrinsic interest in the matter.

I obtained the drug compound required for the 'operation', and I consulted with Tony again and gleaned all that he had been told by the most co-operative Doctor Sargant. I also interviewed my choice of anaesthetist. As well as that, I briefed my secretary, Therese McBryan. At this stage I was hopeful that our application to the court in order to have Meehan seen by our retinue would be successful.

I also consulted the Roussel Laboratories at Columbus House, Wembley Park, London. They gave me several good book references. Many drugs had been tried in attempting to loosen tongues—perhaps the best known being Ethyl Alcohol—in vino veritas. Individual reactions to such drugs may vary to such an extent that it would be difficult to delineate such hard and fast guidelines as to the required dosage. Similarly, the 'lie-detector', or Polygraph, has been shown to be unreliable in detecting whether or not the person it is applied to is, or is not, telling the truth. This machine relies on simultaneous traces taken of the pulse, respiration, blood pressure, heartbeat and the like—which can alter when a lie is told.

I have been present when such a test was carried out in the 1970s in the case of a man called Boyle, who was wrongly charged with attempted murder of two youths by running a car at them. Having been sentenced to ten years by Lord Johnston at Glasgow High Court he consulted me for his appeal. He won his appeal and the lengthy ten years' sentence was quashed. The incident had taken place in Plains, Lanarkshire, and the polygraph experiment which I had done—while he was out on bail for his appeal—in my office, convinced the American expert I had engaged to perform the exercise that there could be no doubt whatsoever of Boyle's total innocence.

The technique is often used in psychiatry in the treatment of traumatic neurosis. The ethical considerations of using such techniques have to be seriously considered and this is why I had the full, informed and written consent of Meehan.

After the Governor of Barlinnie Prison refused my reasonable request, I wrote to the Scottish Secretary—again without success. Undaunted, I prepared the petition. The circumstances in this matter were without Scottish precedent.

The following is from the official record, and reads:

Patrick Connelly Meehan presented a petition to the Nobile Officium of the High Court of Justiciary, in which he averred: '

(1) That the petitioner has been charged with the murder of Mrs Rachel Esther Ross at Ayr on 6th July 1969. He is entirely innocent of the crime charged and was not associated with its perpetration in any way whatsoever.

(2) That the petitioner is anxious to leave nothing undone which may ensure his rightful acquittal and desires to be questioned on every aspect and detail of the crime while he is under the influence of sodium pentothal and methedrine, commonly called "the truth drug".

(3) That the petitioner through his legal advisers requested the Governor of H.M. Prison, Barlinnie, where he is detained, to make arrangements for such an examination to be carried out. His request was conveyed to The Scottish Home and Health Department, but by letter dated 23rd September 1969 the said Department refused it.

(4) The petitioner is therefore deprived of the right to do all he can to try to secure his acquittal and establish his innocence and craves your Lordships to ordain the Governor of H.M. Prison, Barlinnie, to make facilities available for such an examination.

It is proposed that the said drug would be administered by Dr J. Anthony Grogan, police surgeon at Blantyre, Lanarkshire, and his medical assistant, in the presence of Joseph Beltrami, solicitor, and his secretary, and any representative of the Crown who desires to be present. It is also proposed that the questioning and also the answers made by the petitioner whilst under the influence of the said drug should be recorded, both in shorthand and by tape recorder.'

The prayer of the petition was:

May it therefore please your Lordships to ordain the Governor of Barlinnie prison to permit the said Dr J. Anthony Grogan and others to enter the prison for the purpose of administering the said drug to the petitioner; and to provide facilities for administering the said drug and for setting up the proposed recording device, or to do further or otherwise in the premises as to your Lordships shall seem proper.

Fairbairn was on holiday in Italy when the matter was called in Edinburgh and I instructed the most capable Ranald Sutherland QC, now Lord Sutherland of our High Court. The Crown objected to the Application because it contended that the results of the examination would not be admissible in evidence and so had no evidential value. The Crown also contended that statements by the accused should be made with a sound and sober mind and not by way of interrogation, albeit voluntarily.

We argued that had the petitioner (Meehan) been on bail (as Boyle had been) then there would be nothing to prevent such an examination. We argued that judicial declarations were allowed in evidence, as also were replies to caution and charge—so why not this?

The Lord Justice General Clyde, Lord Cameron and Lord Guthrie came to give their opinion, the gist of which was that information obtained by this proposed method could not constitute competent evidence to lay before the jury. Such evidence would only confuse the jury and make their task more difficult. They went on to quote:

> It is one of the fundamental principles of the criminal law of Scotland that the courts have striven to secure that both the prosecution and the defence have an equally full and fair opportunity to lay before the jury through the mouths of witnesses the facts on which they respectively found.
>
> It is also the exclusive function of the jury, after hearing witnesses speaking to these facts, and having their evidence tested by cross-examination, to determine which witnesses they believe. They do so not merely by hearing what the witnesses say, but by the judging of their demeanour when they say it.
>
> The accused is free to go into the witness-box if he chooses, but only if he chooses. It has never been competent for the defence to avoid the giving of evidence by the accused by leading evidence of the accused having denied his guilt extra-judicially to friends or advisors as proof of his innocence.

There was never the slightest possibility of Meehan not giving evidence at his trial and trying to rely on what might have been said by him under the influence of the drug compound.

But our petition was rejected by the court. So far as I know, Tony

Grogan still has the 'truth drug' compound, quite intact, in its 'virgin' state.

As if this wasn't bad enough, the BBC made known their intention to re-enact the circumstances of the Holyrood Crescent shoot-out and the death of Griffiths before our much-awaited trial. In this programme reference was again to be made of Griffiths' criminal record. I was obliged to proceed with all haste to our civil courts with an action for interdict (an injunction in England) prohibiting such interference prior to a major criminal trial. Sheriff Bryden upheld my interdict action and the BBC programme was to be postponed until after the trial.

A further coincidence (this case is full of them) is the fact that Michael Beckham, a producer of the TV documentary which filmed the re-enactment of the last desperate hours of Griffiths was charged with two offences of breach of the peace at Glasgow Sheriff Court arising out of the filming. Would you believe who was instructed by the mighty BBC to tender a plea of guilty on Beckham's behalf?

I duly appeared and my client Beckham was fined the sum of £25 by Sheriff Pirie for, 'Having at Holyrood Crescent conducted himself in a disorderly manner by directing five actors to re-enact certain events leading to the death of Griffiths in Glasgow on 15th July 1969 for the purpose of filming this re-enactment.' The charge went on to say that Beckham caused the actors, under his direction and armed with weapons, to fire shots of blank ammunition in the vicinity of Holyrood Crescent where Griffiths once lived. It was also alleged that one of the actors smashed a pane of glass in the house with a rifle butt, all which caused fear and alarm to residents and passers by.

Beckham was fined a further £25 for having on 26 August near Possil Road and in the Round Toll Bar, conducted himself in a disorderly manner by directing one of the actors armed with a shotgun, rifle and bandoliers, to re-enact the actions of Griffiths in the same bar on 15 July. The charge went on to say that Beckham, on being asked to leave the premises, refused to do so.

Beckham was filming abroad at the time of the calling and the matter was dealt with in his absence.

My interdict action against the BBC craved the court to prohibit the screening of the reconstruction. I averred that Meehan had been charged with the Ayr murder virtually along with the deceased Griffiths, in view of the terms of the Crown Office Statement, which I quoted. In other words, I had a double task—the defence of Meehan and that of a dead man as well!

With this latest success with the interdict I wondered what could possibly happen next.

At this point I had only been on the case for about seven or eight weeks. One should remember that at this time I had a rather busy practice to run and couldn't simply drop everything in order to concentrate on this important case—although I was firmly convinced, more than ever, particularly because of the truth drug development, that Meehan had to be, and was, entirely innocent. I had dealt with many, many clients in the past and one's experience can be invaluable in assessing a client's credibility and reliability. I knew that he wasn't deceiving me—he wasn't that good.

Oh, yes, the police had told me that Meehan was an actor and could take in most people—but I suppose they had to say that in view of his repeated and vociferous protestations of innocence from the rooftops. Understandably, he was demanding and would send me lengthy letters, daily. I confess I didn't read them all but delegated the job of sifting through them to my capable secretary. She would underline important points in red.

So I knew that Meehan and Griffiths were as innocent as I was. It followed, as night follows day, that the two persons responsible were still at large. I decided to go to the Glasgow 'underworld' in search of assistance. . . .

7

I had many influential clients in Glasgow who knew, generally, what was happening there as well as elsewhere in Britain. Indeed, some of them knew what was going to happen before it happened.

Murder was a big crime—and 'tie-up' jobs were rare and would seldom be contemplated by your average crook, because of their inherent danger. I felt that I had no choice but to go to the underworld for help. The police would not allow me to take advantage of their own formidable grapevine of information, passed on by their numerous informers. I was clearly on one side of the divide, the forces of law and order on the unreachable other.

The Scottish underworld consists of many different villains, of varying degrees of criminal involvement, who had their own grapevine of what was happening and who might just give me the help I needed. Or even just the reassurance that I was right in believing that Meehan and Griffiths could not have carried out the robbery and murdered Mrs Ross.

Many of these denizens of that underworld had mixed bags of convictions, having served sentences for dishonesty, breaches of the peace, robbery and extremely wanton violence. No one, perhaps, more than I, knows of their past unsuccessful clashes with the law. It is what brings them to my door in the first place.

I am often asked how I feel, deep down, when I am with such hybrid and often psychopathic characters—and usually alone. I must confess that I have never given this much thought, as I consider that they need me more than I need them.

Not a few of them, of course, are formidable people, built like the back end of a bus and carrying ugly tell-tale scars. I have often thought that the more scars visible, the less daunting the person who bears them—perhaps too often a loser. One old client personified this—Victor 'Scarface' Russo, who had, as the underworld would say, a face like a hot cross bun, but who was certainly not the most frightening of people I have come across in my waiting room.

I must have interviewed more potentially dangerous clients than most, yet only once was I attacked. My assailant—all five feet five inches of him—threw unexpected punches at me and tried to gouge out my right eye as I passed him in busy Ingram Street on my way to Glasgow Sheriff Court.

Earlier, my attacker had watched his wife being sentenced to two years' imprisonment at Glasgow High Court and he was, understandably, shattered—and entirely at odds with the law and with anyone in any way involved with it. He had recognised me, although I did not know him. In any event, he was quickly arrested and taken away. It turned out that he had also caused a good deal of damage at the High Court building as part of his protest. Because of the strike at that time of sheriff clerks, when no courts were able to sit, he was not brought to justice—much to my relief.

Only on a few occasions have clients tried to browbeat or dominate me and decide the way in which their trials should be tackled—but they are shown the door. Lawyers are agents and act for and on behalf of clients, but they should never be puppets on a string, or manipulated by clients.

Generally, I have had a reasonable relationship with those underworld *cognoscenti* over a period of some 30 years in practice. Lately, however, I have experienced more difficulties with sallow teenage youths than from fully grown and formidable adults who have much less to prove to the world at large.

It may, of course, be the fact that I am over six feet in height myself, heavily built and was brought up in Glasgow's 'Briggait' area that deters some—and finds me not too fearful in situations where the end result of a case has been unfavourable for a client.

On Meehan's behalf, I now went in search of some of the leading figures in the city's underworld—such as Colin 'Coalie' Beattie, whose territory was the Partick area of the city. Colin is a giant of a man, with one murder/culpable homicide acquittal and a number of convictions for violence—but nothing for dishonesty. I have known him for nearly 30 years and always found him to be a most respectful, obliging and mannerly person to deal with as a client.

In the Govan territory, I sought out people like 'Whispering' Smith, who had been acquitted of two murders . . . and the fighting 'Herritys from Hell'.

Then there was the sly, devious and dangerous John Edgar, from Bridgeton—a man feared by the same underworld and distrusted by most. But he, too, was in a position to confirm Meehan's innocence. I always found it uncanny how Edgar, who died in the early 'eighties, had so much knowledge of his fellow criminals, the length and breadth of the country. Edgar, by the way, fancied himself as a witness, an actor of some quality in the witness box, which held no fears for him.

I contacted more and more of those underworld characters for assurances of my client's innocence—for the merest prospect of being strung along by Meehan worried me dreadfully. No one wishes to be seen as gullible or naive by the throng.

I realised that I had been fortunate to have built up such an extensive criminal law practice at that time, and I had a complete all-round choice of criminals to tap for information. In those days there were only ten lawyers or so concentrating on criminal work in the country. Now walk into any back street and you will find a solicitor's office, or, more likely, sub-office. Instead of ten, this figure could be multiplied by 100. Nowadays, due to the dispersal of people to the many housing schemes, there are financial barriers to travelling into town to consult a solicitor. As a result, small legal offices have mushroomed all over—in main streets, side-streets, back-alleys, dead-ends and lanes.

Today, I would not be in the same advantageous position of having such important and knowledgeable clients all over the city—and in other cities, too—if I had not built up such a large practice down the years.

My raid on Glasgow's underworld did bear fruit. Most of those I consulted assured me that Meehan was innocent. Even a particular CID officer indicated that I was 'not wasting my time'.

It was something I had not done before—seek out and mix with clients. As a student, and then as a young, recently qualified lawyer, I would go into bars for the odd bottle of Guinness stout. But, as I became better known, I stopped doing that. Now I prefer to eat and drink alone and use the time to sort out the problems of others in my mind.

Strangely enough, Meehan, very much an underworld character himself, with contacts galore, never at any time suggested that I should take the unusual course of going to the underworld for confirmation of his innocence. Perhaps he could not bear the thought that I was not utterly convinced of his not being guilty or involved in the murder.

Anyway, stretched as I was at that time, I broke my golden rule: I went into pubs at night for casual chats with clients I knew would be there. Some came to my office on other business and I questioned them. Others I sent for. My approach did not vary—each time I asked: 'What do you know of the Ayr murder? I think I am representing a totally innocent man.' I did not need to mention Meehan by name. Or the fact that he was my client. The extensive media coverage had seen to that. Everyone knew of my intense involvement.

I readily admit that I received a lot of co-operation, perhaps because an old Jewish lady had lost her life in horrific circumstances. In the vernacular of the underworld, her death was a 'diabolical liberty'. The strictures regarding 'grassing' were transcended by the enormity of the well-planned crime—and the way it had gone terribly wrong.

Again and again, the names of Ian Waddell and Andrew Dick kept cropping up. These were names that hitherto had been unknown to me, which I thought was strange. I was told where they lived in Glasgow's East End and that they were related. I had them described to me but, at that stage, I was none the wiser.

In the end, and in order to try and remove, once and for all, the thought that I was being led up the garden path, I decided to approach one more important source of information—the best. I decided to speak again to one of my special clients, Arthur Thomson.

I was aware that he not only knew Meehan, but that they had been convicted together of a safe-blowing in the early 'fifties at a village called Beauly in Ross-shire. I was confident that Thomson would not mislead me in a matter that was as important to me as this was.

Arthur Thomson came to my office in response to a telephone call. I remember looking at him across my large desk and saying: 'I must know the truth. I have had such misleading information about this case. Am I representing a man who is as entirely innocent as he claims? I need some reassurance.'

Thomson was an impressive-looking figure—about five feet ten inches tall and weighing about 12 stones. He was well-built, in a not-so-obvious way—his suits were well cut and sober, his ties and shirts conservative. Distinguished-looking and slightly older than I, his face displayed small marks of bygone conflicts. He had more acquittals to his name than most. I knew that Thomson would know the correct answer to my question—or was it plea?

Thomson looked at me with those gun-metal eyes of his and said firmly, 'Meehan had nothing at all to do with the Ayr murder, nor had Griffiths.'

That was it. Thomson was a man of few words—nothing more need be said, nor would it. Any lingering doubts in my mind were well and truly expelled. I was now certain beyond a peradventure.

And, suddenly, it hit me. What a responsibility now lay on my shoulders—the defence of an innocent man believed by those who mattered to be as guilty as sin and as cunning as a fox! That thought brought on one of many cold sweats I was to have over this case. I didn't recall ever having required to adopt such an unorthodox approach in the past, but Meehan's case was very special and of a strictly 'one-off' variety.

On reflection, my approach was also dangerous. What would have happened had I been told that he was guilty and that he had deceived me throughout? I may well have required to withdraw from the case. But my instincts, senses and experience told me that I merely wished to have confirmation of his innocence and did not really think that there was any danger of having his guilt spelled out to me.

It may be interesting to note and understand the position of a solicitor vis a vis 'guilty' or 'not guilty' assertions by his client. It is never my practice to ask a client if he committed the crime with which he was charged. When I take instructions from a client I am conscious of the fact that I am his agent, not his confessor. I normally say, 'How do you plead to the charge, Guilty or Not Guilty?'

If the client says, 'Guilty', then I would discuss the charge, take a note of his background and any mitigating factors, and try to obtain enough information to explain his conduct or actions when the case came to court. Later, I would represent him in his plea of guilty and try to have him as fairly and reasonably dealt with as all the prevailing circumstances might allow.

If, on the other hand, the client tells me that he is pleading not guilty then I accept that fact, and start the preparation for his eventual trial.

As I said, I am merely his agent and even if I think that he might be guilty, such thoughts are irrelevant as I am neither judge nor jury in his

*case. I might well be the first to point out to him that his explanation for
certain facts is hardly feasible and unlikely to be accepted. I would give him
the reasons for my conclusions. On occasions I might well try to convince
him to change his plea and avoid undue embarrassment to himself (as well
as myself). It would be proper in such circumstances to point out that judges
often take a more severe view of a person continuing to deny guilty
involvement in the face of incontrovertible Crown evidence.*

*In the hypothetical situation of a client, in the course of preparation for
trial, stating that he was pleading not guilty, coming clean, as it were, and
stating that he had done the evil act, one's duty is clear.*

*Solicitors have duties both to the court and client. The client can be
advised to seek advice elsewhere—in short, to go to another firm of
solicitors. Alternatively, as the prosecution require to prove the case beyond
reasonable doubt—the onus of so-doing resting on the shoulders of the
Crown—the solicitor could continue to act, with the view of putting the
Crown to the test.*

*The client would be told that, in the latter case, I could not put forward a
substantive defence (such as alibi, self-defence etc.) nor, indeed, could I call
him to the witness box in his own defence. If I did this, in view of the
knowledge I had of the client's position, I would be very much instrumental
in assisting the client to commit perjury, as I could reasonably assume that
he would deny (wrongly) the charge.*

*In such a situation, it would be only fair to advise the client that his
position might be prejudiced, subject to these strictures, and that the wiser
course would be to go elsewhere (making him understand just why this was
necessary) or, indeed, if he saw fit, to defend himself. It would be quite
improper for a solicitor to put forward a defence to a charge, knowing from
the client that this defence was false.*

*Indeed, I go further. If a solicitor ascertained from precognoscing defence
witnesses that the defence to be advanced was bogus and false, then his
position would be the same as earlier explained. He could not continue to
advance such a bogus or false defence, bearing in mind the knowledge he had
gleaned from the witnesses.*

However, back to Meehan's guilt or innocence. . . .

I remember stopping at traffic lights one day. A driver alongside
me, a complete stranger, said, 'You've had it this time, Beltrami—
Meehan is as guilty as sin.' I remember thanking him for his encourag-
ing words. There was a great deal of pressure on me at this time—
and, as we shall see, for many, many years thereafter.

The word was now out and I remember the late John Swandells and his brother-in-law waiting for me at Glasgow Sheriff Court. John Swandells was a violent psychopath with several lengthy prison sentences in his record. He was built like a miniature 'King Kong' and had a heart to match. Such was his record that, in the late 'seventies, when he was charged with the theft of a suitcase from Glasgow's Central Station it was taken at solemn sheriff and jury level. The jury, possibly out of sympathy at the paucity of the 'haul' of the well-used suitcase's contents—or, perhaps, because my client was clearly going downhill fast in health and ambition—found the charge Not Proven. The fact that bail had been refused on the grounds of his bad record and that, as a result, he had already served three months as an untried prisoner may have brought some consolation to the Crown.

Swandells and his relation were in a car parked outside the building. As I left, they called me over and told me that Meehan was entirely innocent of the Ayr murder and that I should get on to two men—Ian Waddell and a man called Andrew Dick. Those names again! Two of my Runyonesque clients, 'Dead-eye' McKenna and the 'Aga Khan' (George McCann had a definite resemblance to the late Aga) were consulted. Both, at that time, were quite adept at the art of pick-pocketing or theft (without violence other than perhaps a minor push) from the person. Each had likeable qualities including a keen sense of humour. They knew only of Waddell although they placed Dick somewhere in the obscure background.

The 'Aga' died some time ago and 'Dead-eye', having long since given up his 'craft', now survives on his snooker and pool winnings – thus the nickname.

A fair number of my clients were consulted by me and they were all quite glib about the name of Ian Waddell but, as to the second man, there wasn't the same certainty. Andrew Dick's name was mentioned and a man called Phillips was also mentioned. It was suggested that Dick had been involved but called off at the last minute and was replaced by Phillips. I was told that Waddell and Dick had planned the whole operation. This prior knowledge of Dick's withdrawal proved to be spot on, although it was years later before I was able to latch on to the true identity of Waddell's accomplice.

This was not the first, or, indeed, the last, time that I would 'pray in aid' the uncannily accurate criminal grapevine in this case. Indeed, the CID depend on it for many arrests and many of them would have known by then that the wrong man was in Barlinnie prison.

8

As one detective told me, 'Waddell's name is mentioned a lot.' A client said, 'The dogs in the street are barking the names of Waddell and Dick. Even they know Meehan's innocent. The police must know, too.'

Yes, this case was the talk of the proverbial underworld 'steamie' and I was the listener supreme.

The fact that so many persons, all being seen separately and independently, should be coming up with the name of Waddell was staggering.

I was soon to find out that Ian Waddell was then a fairly small-time crook, possibly involved in his first 'tie-up' job. But there was a second man and as to his identity the position was not nearly so clear. I detected a certain reticence as to the name of Waddell's accomplice. I began to be sure that he must be a 'heavy'. People seemed to be afraid to be specific about who the second man had been.

I then learned that Waddell had been taken in for questioning about the murder, several days before Meehan had been arrested. He had paid a lawyer a good deal of money for the simple task of accompanying him to the police station.

He had paid a lot of money to a lawyer? I knew that Waddell had never worked in his life. How did he have such cash? And the police must have known something, to bring him in for questioning in the first place.

When I next saw Meehan, I told him that I thought the crime for which he was charged had been committed by a man called Ian Waddell and his friend, Andrew Dick. Meehan didn't bat an eyelid. But this information seemed news to him and he asked me who they were and how I came to know. I told him that, as luck would have it, I had learned that Ian Waddell was at that time in Barlinnie Prison on charges of housebreaking. In fact, he was in the same untried prisoners' wing at Barlinnie as Meehan was.

Meehan said, grimly, that he would speak to Waddell at the first available opportunity.

At around this time I wrote once more to the Crown Office, requesting that the trial should not take place in Ayr. I enclosed Press photographs of the scenes I had witnessed outside Ayr Sheriff Court when Meehan had appeared there. Indeed, I had learned that at least one person had been charged with kicking Meehan and had been fined the princely sum of £5.

The trial did eventually take place in Edinburgh—in a courtroom that had seen so many famous trials. But these historic trials did not interest me—my mind was fully taken up with the prospects of success and the nagging possibility of unthinkable failure. These were most anxious times, indeed. Even lawyers, who seldom discussed business with me, were asking about the state of the evidence. Several strangers stopped me in the street, such was the prevailing interest.

Meehan's letters became more and more interesting after Waddell had been locked up in the same prison wing. One such letter was quite revealing, relating to the trip to Stranraer.

We left Stranraer, driving off in the direction of Girvan. We came to a large hotel several miles north of Stranraer. This hotel stands facing a derelict Ministry of Defence camp. On the same side as the hotel, about 150 to 200 yards along the main road, there is a cut-in, leading to a couple of abandoned nissen huts.

Griffiths drove the car into the cut-in and put out the lights. He said the hotel was still too well-lit for him to have a look around. We both got out and walked back along the main road towards the hotel. Facing it was an open gate leading into the derelict camp. We went into the camp and stood watching the hotel.

We hadn't been there long when we heard the National Anthem being played and Griffiths said. 'That's them finishing up at midnight.' There seemed to be quite a lot of people in the hotel and it sounded as though a party was going on. There was a bus standing in the car park and about 15 or 20 minutes later—after the anthem—people started

coming out and driving away. The bus drove off towards Stranraer.
We stood there for about another hour and still people came out, from
time to time, and drove off in cars.

The front of the hotel was so well lit up that Griffiths said he'd
rather wait until some of the lights went out in the larger window,
which looked on to the car park. As we were standing there a large
German Shepherd dog came running from the hotel grounds and
across the road into the camp where we were. A man came out and
called out to the dog to come. I was fondling the dog as the man
called and it bounded away towards him.

When it came to about 1.30 a.m. two women and a man, or it might
have been three women, came out and walked along the road south-
wards and entered a house about 200 yards away. I got the impression
that these people were staff.

Just about this time a number of young men came out of the hotel
and sat in a car, waiting for someone to come out. The someone
seemed to be holding up the departure and they shouted, pressing the
car hooter repeatedly. Whoever it was came out and the car drove off
towards Stranraer.

The front lights of the hotel had now dimmed and Griffiths decided
to have a look around. I told him I'd stay in the camp, and, since there
was a quarter moon, I'd move back, as the light of the moon was
getting stronger. I moved further back into the camp grounds and
stood watching. I also noticed a light on in an upstairs room of a house
and I could see a man in the room. The man was moving about in the
room and I thought, 'He's up late.'

(Meehan supplied diagrams.) The letter continued:

I waited in the camp for Griffiths to return and eventually he did so.
He told me he had no success. We then returned to the car and set off
for Glasgow. On our way Griffiths told me that he had forced open a
couple of cars but didn't get anything. He said he had tried to force the
door of one vehicle—I think he said it was a van. The handle had
come off the door. He definitely damaged a couple of cars in the car
park.

The hotel people will verify that you couldn't interfere with the cars
that were interfered with unless the front of the hotel was in darkness.
On that particular night the hotel front windows were lit up until well
after midnight. One of the cars damaged by Griffiths was hard up
against the front window.

Anyway, we were passing through Ballantrae when Griffiths spotted
a Jaguar car parked outside a small hotel. He said he'd have to get

something, as his cash was low. He turned into the side and left me sitting in the car. He returned about 20 minutes later and said he'd had no luck. I can't recall if he'd said he'd damaged the Jaguar.

We then got underway for Glasgow and we did not stop again until a few miles south of Kilmarnock when I spotted a girl on the main road who seemed to be in distress.

All this information was checked out by us and found to be correct and accurate. We found the man with the dog, the staff who had gone into a house nearby, and the man in the other house. We cited the proprietor of the hotel, The Lochryanhall, and some of the party guests. We also traced the owner of the Jaguar which had, in fact, been damaged in Ballantrae.

There could be little doubt that what Meehan said in his lengthy epistles was correct. The difficulty about our alibi—and the Crown took full advantage of this—was that the time taken for the robbery and murder could not be exactly pinpointed.

Ross was extremely vague on matters of time and this was to plague us at the trial. Even the girls Burns and Smith were unaware of times, although Ross did say that shortly after the raiders left it was 'quite full daylight'. It is to be considered that the pick-up of Burns and Smith—not at full daylight, but well before—must have occurred before the raiders finished and not after, as the Crown tried to argue.

This again would have meant that Meehan and Griffiths did their 'Sir Galahad act'—if the accused were guilty—in the full knowledge that they intended to carry out a serious robbery in the not-too-distant Ayr, shortly after broadcasting their presence nearby! Yet the car approached the lay-by from the south—not the north.

In another letter to me Meehan claimed to have been speaking to prisoners who were in contact with Waddell in the prison. The picture I was given was that on 6 July Waddell told a prisoner, McCusker, that he, Waddell, needed an alibi. Dick had been there and suggested that Waddell say that he was playing cards in a house. Later Waddell had given Dick the money to hire a car, after which Dick, McCusker, Waddell and his girlfriend all celebrated at the Mill Hotel, Rutherglen. Meehan was told that Dick was not involved in the robbery, because he had had to borrow money from Waddell to pay for drinks at the Mill Hotel.

McCusker went on to tell Meehan that the robbery was over and done with by about 1.30 a.m. (at which time Meehan and Griffiths were still at the Lochryanhall, about 50 miles away) and that the other man (not Waddell) went to fetch the getaway car. On the way to the car this other man was stopped by a policeman and questioned as to his movements. The man made an excuse that he had been through at the Orange Lodge parade in Irvine.

I was loath to accept this hearsay information from a prisoner who would speak to my client but not to me. After all, one of the robbers being stopped by a policeman near to the bungalow?—surely I should have heard of this from the police.

If the information were so, then the getaway car must have belonged to the second man, because Waddell had given Dick the cash to hire a car on the late afternoon of 6 July.

Another Meehan letter claimed that Waddell had told McCusker while on exercise that he had been 'spotted', or seen, at the house. Waddell's alibi given to the police must be false. He told them that he had spent the night of 5/6 July at the house of Donald Carmichael in Glasgow's East End. Meehan was confident that Donald Carmichael's wife, Martha, could be broken in the witness box. His confidence was based on information supplied from the prisoners, McCusker in particular.

It was now patently clear that Waddell would require to be incriminated at the trial and that we would have to break his false alibi.

Meehan in another letter told me that the second man was now a G. McCawley. I knew of this man but he also proved to be a red herring—as did Dick and Phillips. But the information was coming in hard and fast. Some of it was quite misleading and contradictory and I began to wonder if Meehan were being strung along with the aim of hopelessly confusing me.

There was also mention made of Waddell giving a public house chargehand, nicknamed 'Big Skip', a wad of notes when he saw two CID officers enter the bar where he had been drinking. 'Big Skip' was a good friend of Waddell's, apparently.

I knew a 'Big Skip', having earlier defended him at a sheriff and jury trial in Glasgow. His name was John Skiverton and he managed the Club Bar in Gallowgate.

Closer to the trial, another letter—these arrived daily—told me that most certainly the second man (the consensus at that time was that he was Sam Phillips from Tollcross, a man I was desperately trying to trace) had been stopped by two policemen in a police car in Ayr on the night of the murder and questioned by them. I was still sceptical about this information dredged from Barlinnie but decided that I should do something, if only to cover my own back.

I phoned the Ayr CID requesting to speak to Superintendent Struthers. I spoke to a Detective Constable Gall, making two requests. The first was to have photographs shown to certain witnesses. The second was more important—I asked to be given the names of the two police officers who, in the early hours of the morning of the murder, had stopped and given a lift to someone in Racecourse Road, Ayr, near the bungalow.

This information was not known to Detective Constable Gall and I told him to check on it and come back to me if there was any reliability to be attached to the information. No one ever came back to me prior to the trial, or, indeed, after the trial and I assumed that no such event had happened. With justification, I felt that this information about a man being stopped by two policemen near the bungalow was simply part of a wild goose chase which only served to prolong my investigations.

Round about this time I received the long-awaited indictment and could not help but think that if my information were correct about the second man being stopped by two police officers, then these officers must surely have been put on the prosecution list of witnesses. They were not, so I discounted this matter in its entirety.

Seven years later I discovered officially that Police Officers McNeill and Hepburn of the Ayr Constabulary had, in fact, picked up a man in Racecourse Road. This man had been McGuinness, although he had not given that name.

The time had been 4.30 a.m. and the place was Racecourse Road, just round the corner from Blackburn Place and the murder bungalow. The man had been walking north and had told the officers that he was going to the bus station in Ayr to catch a bus to Glasgow.

These officers had later been shown a photograph of McGuinness and identified him. The man had said that he had been to the Orange Walk in Irvine and had got drunk there. The officers had then given him a lift to Ayr bus station. Somehow their report had not reached the proper channels, had never reached the Procurator Fiscal in Ayr, and Struthers had no knowledge of its existence. How matters would have changed had I been given this information on the telephone—or anywhere for that matter—seven years earlier!

Meanwhile, that font of information (McCusker) did not wish to speak to me, but I was soon to receive a letter from a Barlinnie prisoner who did.

Robert McCafferty asked to see me at once. The matter concerned Meehan. McCafferty told me of a conversation he had had with Waddell while on exercise in 'C' Hall. Waddell told him (and this was ten days before Meehan's trial was due to start) that Waddell and not Meehan had carried out the robbery. McCafferty went on to say that Waddell had told him that he felt sorry for Meehan, who was being 'set up'. McCafferty agreed to give evidence.

Another prisoner, William McIntyre, also asked to see me. McIntyre told me that he had been approached months earlier by Andrew Dick. He had been invited to join Dick in a robbery in Ayr. At first McIntyre had agreed to go along with this and had met Waddell in Dick's house. The proposed crime had been discussed there, and details of a 'tie-up', job, involving two elderly persons, were bandied about. On hearing these details McIntyre had decided to renege. He went on to say that he had stayed up on the morning of 6 July in his own home with Dick, to give the latter an alibi, and that he was later given £10 for his services. *Dick's alibi had in fact been thoroughly checked by the CID, who had found it to be foolproof.*

Both these prisoners had criminal records and were awaiting trial on other matters. Not the best of credentials—but I was desperate and had to grasp at any straw.

By now the indictment was out and trial put down for Tuesday, 21 October. Quickly, I had all the Crown witnesses seen and statements taken from them, and still not a scintilla of evidence about anyone being picked up by the police in the early hours of 6 July, at Racecourse Road.

The Crown had to have something extra—and it had!

9

Six weeks after the Griffiths shoot-out, Superintendent Cowie had come back from leave and had a discussion with Detective Superintendent Struthers.

Mention was made of pieces of old paper having been found in Griffiths' car-coat pocket. This paper was brown and white in colour. Cowie said he remembered seeing something similar on 7 July when he had examined the safe at the murder bungalow. Detective Inspector Cook, of the Glasgow Forensic Department, and Cowie examined the safe again on 21 August and removed brown-coloured paper from one of its drawers, as well as a diary. Pieces of brown paper were also removed from the floor of the cupboard in which the safe had been housed.

Cook would give evidence saying that the pieces of brown paper from the car coat were similar to the pieces taken from the safe drawers and found on the floor of the safe cupboard. Similar in all respects—microscopically—and that they were all old and disintegrated easily. They also matched in colour and shade.

So far as the pieces of white paper found in the car coat, these were similar in colour, texture and in age to the pages of the diary in the right-hand drawer of the safe.

The crunch was that the blue-coloured ink on the tiny pieces of paper was similar in every way to the blue-coloured ink of the lettering in the pages of the diary. In short, in every possible respect, these items matched exactly. Detective Inspector Cook would go on to say that he concluded they had a common origin.

Meehan was astonished at this evidence. I was stunned.

Meehan did not trust the police—as is evidenced by the fact that days after the initial court appearance he received word in the prison that officers would call to collect his suit. Realising, as he thought, that there could be little against him other than the erroneous voice identification—and two sets of coincidences—he feared that something incriminating might be 'planted' in his clothing.

He was sufficiently worried about the possibility to ask two prison officers, Deans and Gaitens, to examine the suit carefully before handing it over to the police. After handing over the suit they told Meehan that it had been thoroughly looked at by them and that if there had been something 'it could only show up under a microscope'. Nothing had been found in the suit. But this was much worse.

The only person who could have denied the presence of such paper in his car coat was Griffiths and his was a voice from the grave. Meehan was more than suspicious about the finding of the tiny tell-tale pieces of paper in the car coat of Griffiths. After studying these witness statements, I was quite crestfallen. Meehan wrote to me as follows:

> I have tied myself to Griffiths. The Crown will argue that my statement is a denial that Griffiths was involved in the crime. The Crown are, therefore, going to point to the paper in the pocket of Griffiths as evidence against him, their case being that evidence against one is evidence against both.
>
> The Crown argue 'association' when the 'associate' is not present to explain the paper in his pocket. I do not think the nature of the evidence justifies the Crown demanding from me an explanation for what they say was found on Griffiths. The Crown are trying to use evidence against one accused to corroborate the case against the other. Am I to sit in the dock with an accused who cannot communicate with the court, counsel or jury? Can we apply to the High Court to have a spiritual medium in the dock just in case Griffiths decides to get in touch?

On the evening of Sunday, 12 October, Glasgow's head of CID, Chief Superintendent Tom Goodall, collapsed in his garden and died. He had suffered a massive heart attack. The suddeness of his death, a man in his prime, shocked us all. He was to have been a Crown witness, speaking about telephone conversations he had had with Griffiths, after Meehan's arrest. Griffiths had told Goodall that both he and Meehan were innocent.

I had always been an admirer of Goodall and had gone to see him in his famous corner office in Turnbull Street to express my concern about the case on some three occasions. In particular, I saw him after the body blow when the paper evidence came to light. I reiterated my view of Meehan's innocence and yet he could be convicted of this heinous crime, one totally out of character for him.

Goodall had a somewhat lean and hungry look. He had a fantastic determination in his inexorable pursuit of criminals. He was known as 'the Fox', for obvious and well-deserved reasons. I couldn't talk to Struthers or Cowie as I could Goodall—and always 'off the record'.

I tried to draw information out of him, because his grapevine contacts were better than mine. In other words, he knew the score. He didn't say much on the last occasion I saw him alive—simply, 'Don't worry too much'—as I clearly was. 'In my opinion, the verdict will be Not Proven at least.' I had been less despondent when I left him.

As I attended the Linn Crematorium I thought that he, too, had been uneasy about this case. He had known Meehan for many years and knew that there was a total absence of violence in his make-up. 'That's not his style,' he would say.

I felt that Goodall's death was yet another blow to Meehan's chances. It was said by some that Tom Goodall had been responsible for the nickname 'Tank', as in 'Tank' McGuinness. Yet another coincidence?

It may be apocryphal, but years earlier he had gone to a South Side bar to detain McGuinness on a warrant. McGuinness was drinking at the bar with friends when he was told by Goodall that he was taking him in. In the process of drinking a pint, McGuinness appealed to Goodall, 'Let me finish my pint first.' Goodall said, 'Tank up, McGuinness, you're not going anywhere, anyway.' He allowed him to finish his pint—and the nickname 'Tank' stayed with him. I prefer the theory earlier expressed by me, that the nickname 'Tank' had to do with his expertise in opening safes.

Back to the pieces of paper . . . and may I say that Ross was to state in his sworn evidence that he did not remember there being any paper in his safe.

At a later trial, of Waddell and Dick, for the Ayr murder and conspiracy, we were to hear from no less a person than Chief Superintendent Joe Beattie from the CID that the clothing of Griffiths [including the car coat] had been searched by two of his officers, Detective Inspector Simpson and Chief

Inspector Brown, and then taken to the Northern police station shortly after the shoot-out. No paper had been found by them. Joe Beattie stated that he was positive that his two experienced and trusted officers would have found paper in any pocket, had there been any. Again, had we had the benefit of his evidence at Meehan's trial, then who knows...?

The exact charges that mattered in the long-awaited Indictment were as follows:

> Patrick Connelly Meehan, prisoner in the prison of Barlinnie, Glasgow, you are indicted at the instance of the Right Honourable Henry Stephen, Lord Wilson of Langside, Her Majesty's Advocate, and the charges against you are that, while acting along with James Griffiths, Flat 29, 14 Holyrood Crescent, Glasgow (now deceased), you did (1) on 20th or 21st June 1969 at the Royal Stewart Motel, Gretna, Dumfriesshire, steal a motor car, registered number MAV 810G containing a camera, two pairs of spectacles, two aluminium chairs, a picnic table, two cushions, a foot pump, a tyre gauge, two torches, twelve coat hangers, two cases, two bottles of wine, a picnic basket and a quantity of clothing, personal papers and documents;
>
> (2) on 6th July 1969 break into the house occupied by Abraham Ross and Esther Rachel Freedman or Ross, his wife, and did strike Abraham Ross on the head with an instrument, punch him on the face and body, strike him on the shoulder and buttock with a sharp instrument and bind him with rope and nylon stockings, all to his severe injury, and did assault said Esther Rachel Freedman or Ross, drag her from her bed, place her on the floor, place a knee on her chest and bind her with rope and nylon stockings, all to her severe injury, and did rob them of £1,800 of money and a number of traveller's cheques, and further you did abandon said Abraham Ross and said Esther Rachel Freedman or Ross bound as aforesaid in said house where they lay without assistance for a period of 30 hours and in consequence thereof said Esther Rachel Freedman or Ross died in Ayr County Hospital, Ayr on 8th July 1969, and you did murder her.

As one must, I gave the Crown intimation of the alibi lodged on behalf of Meehan, as well as confirmation of the fact that I intended to incriminate Ian Waddell and Samuel Phillips for the murder and robbery.

Try as I did, I could not find Andrew Dick, who had clearly disappeared from sight. Not long before the trial's commencement my precognition manager at last managed to trace a Samuel Phillips at 4 Hopeman Road in Glasgow. I told him to report to me just as soon as he'd interviewed Phillips.

This he did. He came to me in the office and said that Phillips had nearly had a heart seizure when the suggestion was made to him of being an accessory in the Ayr murder. I accepted the experience of Michael MacDonald, my office manager, and realised that the second man impeached by us had been a red herring, who, in fairness, could not be called by responsible solicitors. Clearly, this Samuel Phillips had no connection whatsoever with the Ayr murder.

I was still receiving letters from Meehan daily before the trial. One of them, dated 14 October, stated as follows:

> This evening I cornered Waddell and I told him that it was important to my defence to know if the old man (Ross) had been blindfolded. Waddell is most emphatic that the old man was neither blindfolded nor gagged. Waddell said a blanket was thrown over the old man and several times the old man knocked it off and it had to be replaced. Waddell says the old man is definitely lying if he says he was blindfolded.
>
> Waddell says the old man must have known it was daylight when they left as the house lights were turned off by Waddell at dawn and they didn't finally leave until 6 a.m.

The letter went on to say that Waddell told him that the names of Pat and Jimmy were used during the attack. Other letters claimed that Waddell had paid a solicitor a substantial sum of money to be present at his (Waddell's) questioning. 'Such information,' he said, 'would have to be declared by the solicitor to the Inland Revenue. I think the sum was £200. . . Waddell went on to tell me, that the car used in the Ayr robbery was a hired car, not a stolen one.'

Yet another letter stated:

> I have tried a little experiment. I lay on the floor . . . with a sheet over my head and the cell light out. It was day and even with my face to the floor I could still tell it was daylight outside. I tried the experiment with a blanket and I could still tell it was daylight. I could see daylight through the weave of the blanket. I think it would be a good idea to question Mr Ross on this. The old man, says Waddell, must know that it was daylight when they left the house.

A further letter repeated the fact that the names 'Pat' and 'Jimmy' had been used, not 'Pat' and 'Jim'. 'If you can get Ross to admit to the fact that the name used was Jimmy that should help. I never called Griffiths, Jimmy—always, Jim.'

Meehan had conversations with McCusker, McCafferty, McIntyre, Waddell and a number of other inmates. They were now referring to the second man and always used the term, 'Big man' or 'Big fellow'.

Just about a week before the trial I received another lengthy note from my client. It said:

> A prisoner tells me that Waddell is very worried because we have impeached Phillips. Today McCusker said to me that wee McGuinness left the house at 5.30 a.m. to go for the car and was pulled up by the coppers. He (McCusker) said this to me in the presence of another prisoner who comes from Bridgeton and who is friendly with Waddell. McCusker dropped the name 'Wee McGuinness' as if it was a slip of the tongue. It may have been such a slip, but I'm inclined to think that there's a plot afoot to cover up for Phillips. The build of 'Wee McGuinness' was nothing like that of Phillips, although he was known to go in for 'tie-ups'.

So I had yet another name—but by no means that of the 'big man'.

I knew McGuinness. He had been a client of mine, for some years. He was small and slight. I dismissed this information about 'Wee McGuinness'. Indeed, the police had not come back to me to say that they had stopped anyone in Racecourse Road. So I dismissed this aspect as well.

The identity of the second man was well and truly veiled in confusion, rumour and hearsay as I approached the trial date. Waddell's identity seemed to be much more certain. I had him seen, but he was saying absolutely nothing—'pleading the Fifth', as they say.

It was in this late communication from Meehan that the name of McGuinness was mentioned for the very first time. It was discounted by me, as I've said earlier, and for good reason. The description did not fit the pattern weaved in the welter of information supplied from the prison.

I have never had so many details and 'fact' supplied before a trial—red herrings, false trails and mere prison gossip. Indeed, it was difficult to see the wood for the trees.

One must always bear in mind that my business for the three pre-trial months did not consist of purely Meehan, although that is what he wanted. Life went on, as did the daily trials in the Sheriff Court, identification parades, prison visits and so on.

Meehan was now transferred to Saughton Prison in Edinburgh where Nicholas Fairbairn, John Smith and I had a final pre-trial consultation with him. Yes, there were problems, and no bigger one than the pieces of paper—none more than the size of a shirt button—allegedly found in Griffiths' car coat pocket.

At our final meeting we discussed how we'd face up to this important piece of evidence. We decided that there was no proper basis on which to challenge it. We decided that there was nothing we could do to rebut this dangerous evidence.

Had we dared to suggest that the paper had been 'planted' on the deceased Griffiths by the police, the trial judge would certainly have intervened, stating something like 'quite improper' and 'irresponsible tactics'. On whose instructions did we make this scurrilous attack on senior police officers? Had Griffiths told us from the dead? And, 'Meehan was not present, you know, at Holyrood Crescent—he was locked up at the time'.

Such a flare-up would further prejudice Meehan's chances, and they were bad enough as it was.

At the back of my mind, however, I kept the notion of feeling that surely justice would be done—as it was, eventually, but seven long years later. In the meantime, one could only pray.

There was one final matter before the trial. Two Crown witnesses, Mr and Mrs W. Marshall of 4 Blackburn Road, Ayr, had reported to the police that they had seen two men walking eastwards along the south pavement of Blackburn Road and close to Blackburn Place, which was on the corner. They had then gone into Racecourse Road. The men appeared to be tough in appearance and of a type not usually seen in this prosperous part of Ayr. One was, they said, about five feet eight inches in height, the other five feet eleven inches, the former about 40 years old and the latter 25 to 35 years. Neither had identified Meehan at his parade (Meehan had had two parades, one at Turnbull Street and the other at the Northern police headquarters, Maitland Street.)

You will recall that I had phoned Mr Gall at Ayr about these witnesses and requested that they be shown a number of photographs from SCRO (Scottish Criminal Record Office) including those of Waddell and Phillips. It was arranged that this operation would be supervised by Superintendent Struthers and Cowie, with myself in attendance. Although it was duly done, we drew another blank—no identification.

I would have been happier with a proper identification parade but I was unable to get a warrant for this and had to settle for a 'back door' one with SCRO photographs, some of which are not of the best.

The trial court in Edinburgh—Number Three—in the old Scottish Parliament Buildings had, in its day, housed the celebrated trials of Madeleine Smith, charged with murdering her French lover, Pierre L'Angelier, by poisoning, and also that of the unfortunate little Oscar Slater, who was sentenced to death there, reprieved and then served 19 years in prison before the original verdict was quashed by the then new Court of Criminal Appeal, in 1927. Note this was no Royal Pardon, but the judicial quashing of the sentence.

In passing, may I say that Miss Smith was found 'Not Proven'. And, earlier, Tom Goodall had told me that Meehan would get a 'Not Proven', at least. 'Not Proven' is a verdict peculiar only to Scotland, where a jury can return one of three verdicts—Guilty, Not Guilty, or Not Proven. Many years ago in Scotland there were only two verdicts—Proven and Not Proven. Such verdicts are straightforward and need no explanation. Indeed, some of us think the old verdicts—two in number—satisfied logic better than our present three.

Not Proven is a safeguard type of verdict, when it may be considered by the jury that it would be wrong to say the accused was not guilty of the crime but, nevertheless, the Crown had not proved its case to the required standard and satisfaction—proof beyond reasonable doubt. In short, that the case had not been proved to the standards exigible by our law.

There can remain a stigma with a Not Proven verdict—you did it, but we couldn't prove it—but it is extremely useful as an alternative acquittal verdict. For all practical purposes, the effect of each acquittal verdict is the same, in that, be it Not Guilty or Not Proven, the accused can never be re-tried, for the same matter, even in the event of fresh evidence coming to the surface later on.

10

Court Number Three at the High Court in Edinburgh was jammed packed at the start of Meehan's trial. And there was an air of expectancy of high drama.

Below the lofty judge's bench was a large, square table where sat the Clerk of the Court, with his back to the judge. At this table, too, sat the Crown prosecution team of the Solicitor General of the time, Ewan Stewart QC and John H. McCluskey QC, Advocate Depute. They were assisted by the Assistant Crown Agent, Bill Chalmers, and the Procurator Fiscal of Ayr, R. Cruickshank.

Beside them, and to the judge's left, was the defence formation of Nicky Fairbairn and former Labour Cabinet minister and now MP, John Smith. I was there, assisting them, and sitting between them. Michael MacDonald, my office manager, who knew much more about the case than most people, was also there. As the defending solicitor, I had chosen the counsel and would instruct them. Of course, I had Meehan's agreement on this.

Meehan sat in the dock, flanked by two police officers, resplendent in white gloves, and with polished batons drawn at the ready.

I was extremely nervous. I felt that we could snatch a verdict of Not Proven, but not one of Not Guilty. I had never been under such pressure at a trial—even those of a capital nature, where the accused's life was in the balance. But this was more of a challenge than a case. So much depended on what inference the jury might draw from the tiny pieces of paper—without which I would have settled for nothing less than a unanimous Not Guilty, possibly by the Court's direction.

The three rows for the 15 members of the jury were to the judge's right, and, in the Court's well, facing the judge and beyond counsel's table, was the long, narrow dock protected by a wooden barricade about three feet in height. To the left and behind the dock were several rows of oak-panelled seats, quite cushionless, where were the packed Press benches.

The judge's bench—and all eyes were on it, as we awaited the Justice Clerk, second only to the Justice General in seniority—was covered in red felt, with a small table desk, a seat for the shorthand writer, and the inevitable carafe of water and the usual two shining glasses.

Lord Grant (sometimes referred to as Lord 'Grunt') took the bench, preceded by his court attendant, dressed in grey with a white bow tie and a black gown, who, in stentorian tones, called, 'Court, stand.' He carried the Justice Clerk's silver mace in front and ahead of him, which is why he is often called the Macer of Court. We stood at his very command.

Across the table Ewan Stewart pulled himself up to all of his five feet four inches. He had won an MC during the Second World War and was courageous, with a fine perspicacious mind. He looked like, and often lived up to his nickname, 'Napoleon'. His assistant, John H. McCluskey, had been instructed in his first criminal trial by me in 1957.

In 1974, when the fight for justice in the Meehan case had been prominent in the media since the 1969 conviction—and I tried to see to that—John McCluskey, then Solicitor General, and soon to be a Scottish Law Lord, McCluskey of Churchill, was the main speaker at the Scottish Juridical Dinner in Glasgow's City Halls. In the course of his speech he said, 'Why is it that counsel in the main write law books? I have seldom heard of solicitors doing this. Surely it is time that we had the benefit of something like Miscarriages of Justice I have known, *by Joe Beltrami?' This was clever and topical but, I thought, in bad taste, particularly as I happened to be present.*

Many thought that the Meehan campaign was a gimmick, run by us for the purpose of seeking and enjoying the attendant publicity. I shall send Lord McCluskey a complimentary copy of this book, reminding him of his prophetic dinner speech!

On my side of the table, Fairbairn had been my top counsel for some 11 years at this time. We'd been through a number of capital cases together and had never lost a client to the hangman. Witty and sharp, he could digest points quickly and retentively. We had developed a fine understanding, which was to last for many years to come.

John Smith, his junior, was highly intelligent, but my main reason for engaging him was that he was the Member of Parliament for Lanark. I felt that we might require someone in Parliament after the conclusion of this trial. How right I was. (John has since become Shadow Chancellor and is tipped, regularly, to take over the leadership of the Labour Party.)

I do not propose to cover this trial in detail, in the knowledge that many of the salient points are already well-known. In any event, I feel that the true worth of this saga is not in the trial of Meehan itself but in the lengthy aftermath.

In Scottish criminal trials there are no opening speeches by Counsel, as in England, to tell the jury what they hope their witnesses will say. Here we start with the evidence, as we feel that the opening speeches (in England it is normally one speech, because almost invariably the defence waive this right) can be prejudicial to the accused in that prosecution counsel pitch their case at its very highest, often assuming lines of evidence that never emerge.

I have had a number of cases south of the border, in the Crown Courts, and after hearing the Crown's opening speech have often wondered why we were defending the accused in the first place, so much of a foregone conclusion the outcome seemed to be. The jury must also feel the same way and form pre-conceived notions of obvious guilt, based not on one word of evidence but on the sheer oratory of the Crown leaders. Here we save the speeches until after all the evidence, by both Crown and defence.

A prime witness for the prosecution was called early on—Abraham Ross. Small and frail, he was assisted into the high witness box, to the judge's left. Observing Jewish practice, he had carefully placed his black skull cap on his head before taking the oath.

He described the layout of the house, the movements of his wife and himself that fateful evening of 5 July, and then the robbery. He said he and his wife were asleep in their bedroom when he woke up with something coming towards him. He didn't see who or what was coming at him but someone dived right on top of him . . . it was like a horrid nightmare. He then heard his wife Rachel shouting and screaming and realised that it was no bad dream.

Ross found himself on top of his assailant (the smaller of the two men and obviously the person we now know to be McGuinness). He saw that the smaller man was wearing a hood on his head with appropriate slits for eyes and mouth.

The taller man (Ian Waddell, as we now know) had thrown himself on top of Mrs Ross and was hitting her about the face. The smaller man shouted, 'Get this cunt off me, Pat.' So the taller man (Waddell) left Mrs Ross and came over and struck Mr Ross several times with an iron bar. The smaller of the two men also hit him with a blunt instrument. He was then covered again with the blanket. The light was then turned on.

Whenever Ross tried to remove the blanket, he was struck. His hands were then tied behind his back, as were those of his wife. Mrs Ross told Waddell to be careful of her chest as she had recently had an operation there. Mrs Ross was also covered with a blanket. She pleaded for an ambulance. She asked if Abraham were all right and told them to take what they wished and then leave them in peace.

Mr Ross was asked about a wall safe and only eventually told them where the keys to the safe were, under the stairs. The small man took the keys, opened the safe and took the money contents. Although Ross said the contents were nearly £2,000, it was believed that there was much more money than that in the safe.

Both men made a thorough search of the house, which was well and truly ransacked. In Ross's trouser pocket they found cash and American Express traveller's cheques. A gold watch was taken from Rachel's wrist, as well as two rings from her fingers. One of the intruders then found whisky and lemonade, after which they sat drinking and talking.

Mrs Ross again asked for an ambulance and was told by the taller man, 'Shut up, shut up—we'll send for an ambulance.' The 'u' in ambulance was hardly pronounced at all.

At one point Ross thought he heard one say, 'They're not here yet, Jimmy.' He went on to say that it could have been 'Jim' as opposed to 'Jimmy'.

Both Rosses were now tied up very securely—indeed, so much so that they would not be able to free themselves and sound the alarm. They were tied by their ankles as well as their wrists.

The smaller man then left to fetch the getaway car. (*We now know it should have been the taller man [Waddell], but he had the blood of Mrs Ross all over his clothes.*) He was away for some time, causing the taller man some alarm. The ordeal for Abraham Ross did not finish until nine o'clock on the Monday morning (7 July) when their domestic help, Mrs Grant, arrived for work.

The high water mark of Ross's evidence, from the defence point of view, was that he stated that the raiders had Scottish accents, indeed, Glasgow voices. He was positive of this—the most telling point of the first day's evidence. At this stage I was quite confident.

He was then asked about the identification parade at Turnbull Street and said, 'It sounded like the voice at the time—I was kind of sure, but it is very difficult to say with a voice.' He admitted that at the parade he had been sedated and had been very upset. He admitted that he'd only heard one voice at the parade. Asked if he thought he could recognise either of the voices now, he said, 'No, I do not think so.'

At this stage Fairbairn asked leave of the judge to introduce into the court the person we had impeached—Waddell.

At the pleading diet in Ayr Sheriff Court, ten days before the trial, I had intimated our special defence of alibi, stating that Meehan was in Stranraer at the material time, and I had also intimated in writing, as one must, our intention to impeach or incriminate two persons on this matter. Those persons had been named as being Ian Waddell and Samuel Phillips. In the case of a special defence of impeachment or incrimination, the accused pleads not guilty to the charge and states, in addition, that other persons, in this case Waddell and Phillips, were responsible for the crime, and not he.

Ian Waddell had been put on the Crown list of witnesses—he was also on ours. No person by name of Samuel Phillips was cited by us at the trial. Lord Grant agreed—he had little option, in view of our special defence of incrimination—and Waddell was introduced to the court.

He was given a piece of paper with the following words, 'Shut up, shut up—we'll send for an ambulance.' In addition, the words, 'They're not here yet, Jimmy.' On reading out the first note, regarding the ambulance, Ross said, 'It was like the voice, yes.' On being asked if he was sure, he replied, 'I wouldn't say for sure, no.' He was then asked, 'Is it as like the voice as the one you heard at the police station at the time of the parade?' and he replied, 'It sounds something similar.'

Perhaps feeling that the Crown required rescuing, Lord Grant interrupted—'Is your recollection as clear now, three months later, as it was when you went to the parade?'

'No,' said Ross, 'At that time it was fresh.'

He was then asked if the voice could have belonged to either assailant, and replied, 'It is possible.'

Waddell was then brought back in, to repeat the second sentence about 'Jimmy'. Ross said, 'No, it was not.' He then went on, within seconds, 'It could have been.' Ross finished by saying, 'It's guesswork now on my part to try to remember voices.'

Regrettably for us, Ross had no idea how long the robbers had been in his house—he did not even hear them leave. He did say that the two men had been in his house for a considerable time. He said that after they had gone—about ten minutes later—he had shaken off the blanket and it was then full daylight.

He went on to say that he had no recollection of any paper being in his safe, nor could he say if the safe drawers had shelving paper.

(Ross made no mention of his car keys having been taken, nor was he asked, as there was no significance to be attached thereto at this stage—only many years later.)

Ross described the build of the two men as follows (he did not see their faces): 1. Six feet, and 2. smaller than 1.

Mrs Ross was taken to Ayr County Hospital where she was found to be semi-comatose. All she could say was, 'He knelt on my chest.' She became unconscious and died in the early hours of Tuesday, 8 July. She had been trussed up for too long. Had someone phoned an ambulance in a reasonable period of time it is almost certain that she would not have died.

A doctor was called next. He had examined Meehan at Ayr police station on 15 July and had found absolutely nothing 'consistent with Meehan having been involved in a skirmish ten days earlier'.

The court heard about the Kilmarnock lay-by, a statement by Meehan, the Holyrood Crescent shoot-out, finding of the telltale pieces of paper in the car coat of Griffiths, and the disappearance of the Triumph 2000 car.

Police traffic officers spoke of trial-runs and said the distance between Stranraer and Ayr was 52 miles and had been negotiated in one hour and 27 minutes at an average speed of 35 miles per hour.

Irene Cameron, Griffiths' girlfriend, told the court that he had a 'definite English accent' and that, 'No one would mistake it for a Scottish voice.' She added that after news of the Ayr murder had hit the Press, Griffiths continued to drive about Glasgow's busy streets in the Triumph 2000.

The Crown decided that it would try to establish Waddell's alibi—so spiking our impeachment of him—by leading his main alibi witness, Donald Carmichael, a former client of mine.

Carmichael said that Ian Waddell came to his Tollcross home just before midnight on Saturday, 5 July. 'He had been drinking and had a carry-out with him.' He went on to say that he and his wife Martha had had a few drinks with him. 'Waddell asked to stay the night and spent it on my couch. In the morning he was still there.' Carmichael had been interviewed by the CID not long after the murder and had told them exactly what he was now saying.

Carmichael was a short, powerfully built man who had gone prematurely bald. He had a criminal record. He was cross-examined by Fairbairn and did not sound too convincing. He admitted that after giving his initial statement to the police they had phoned him and asked him to call at the station for clarification purposes. This had worried him so much that he had phoned his solicitor, me, at midnight. I well remember the telephone call. He seemed to be extremely agitated and worried. I made an arrangement that he should call to see me on the following afternoon. Regrettably, he did not keep the appointment. As fate would have it, the police phoned him on the following morning and told him that they did not require to see him.

Fairbairn put it to him in cross-examination that the reason he phoned his solicitor at that unearthly hour was—'because you knew your story covering Waddell was false and you were scared of becoming involved.' 'No,' he replied.

Fairbairn came back at him, 'Then why phone Mr Beltrami at midnight?'

The answer given was, 'At any time I have ever been in trouble with the police I always phone Mr Beltrami.'

'But you weren't in trouble,' said Fairbairn, 'You were giving Waddell a genuine alibi, so you say.'

Carmichael said, 'That's right.'

Fairbairn—'Tell the Jury why you saw fit to phone your solicitor out of office hours.'

Carmichael hesitated but was rescued by Lord Grant—'You have been in trouble several times, I gather?'

'Yes.'

'And I imagine you realise that whether you're guilty of an offence or not, a person who is summoned to the police station is always wise to consult his solicitor, and that solicitors always advise their clients to that effect—if they are reputable and able solicitors—and the courts have said frequently that it is always desirable [*this was no longer a question but becoming a statement of fact*] that a solicitor should be present if anybody is summoned to the police station in order to make a statement. Do you realise that?'

A very grateful Carmichael said, 'Yes,' to this somewhat leading question.

Fairbairn, not to be deterred, said, 'Now please tell the jury why you considered on this occasion you were in trouble with the police?'

Carmichael mumbled something about Mr Beltrami having said in the newspapers that Meehan was innocent. He was certainly right in that regard—but it was still no answer to Fairbairn's question which was allowed to remain unanswered. Instead of his wife, Martha, giving evidence, the Crown gave me a medical certificate, stating that she was unfit to attend Court. We were told that Martha Carmichael might become available later on, but, alas, this was not to be the case.

At the subsequent trial of Waddell and Dick, after Meehan's release, both Carmichaels, having been given immunity from prosecution, swore that Waddell had not spent that night at their home and that Carmichael had received a sum of money from Waddell for furnishing the false alibi.

Waddell was on the Crown list of witnesses but was not called by them—they left him for us, knowing that he would not have immunity from subsequent prosecution. When I realised that the Crown would not call Waddell, I sent my office manager, Michael MacDonald, to see him in the nearby cells, to obtain a statement. MacDonald was asked by Waddell what the position would be now if, during evidence, he admitted to the crime. He was told very properly that he would not have immunity as a Queen's witness because the Crown did not propose to call him, but that we, the defence, did.

He said, 'In that case I have nothing to say.'

The mood of the Court was such that I was afraid to speak to Waddell personally because of my close involvement with Meehan. I felt that if I approached him in any way I would be in danger of incurring the savage wrath of the formidable judge. I took no chances and did not speak to Waddell until years later, and at his request.

At this point and at this stage, may I say that there was a dreadful feeling in the courtroom—one that I had never experienced in the past and fortunately never have since. It seemed that anyone on Meehan's side was indeed on the wrong side of justice, law and order.

Had the Crown called Ian Waddell—and, after all, he was on the Crown list of witnesses—he would have enjoyed immunity from prosecution and one could only guess what his attitude would then have been, although his statement to MacDonald gave us a clear indication of that.

When Detective Sergeant Inglis, the officer in charge of the Turnbull Street identification parade, gave evidence he said that Meehan had taken up the number one position for the *first* witness, Abraham Ross. The parade notes confirmed this order. But Meehan called me over to the dock and whispered that Ross was the *last* person to see the parade. He mentioned 'perjury' about the detective's evidence. I went back and gave this information to Fairbairn, but his reaction, like mine, was, 'Does the order matter in any way? First or last, he identified the voice of Meehan.'

I took it to be a simple error, falling short of perjury! I thought that perhaps the parade sheet was made up by Inglis well in advance, but because of Ross's state the order was altered at the last minute and the officer had simply forgotten to record this fact.

11

When the Crown closed its case, we opened by calling Meehan. He was asked right away if he had anything to do with the Ayr murder.

'I was never at any time involved in that murder and robbery, and I never set eyes on that man Ross until I saw him at the identification parade.'

It would be difficult to be more definite and perjink than that. He was in the box for hours and one part of his evidence is indelibly imprinted in my memory. During the skilful 'cross' by the tactically superb Ewan Stewart, Meehan repeatedly refuted his suggestions by speaking of his innocence. Stewart said, 'You are a self-confessed liar, aren't you?'

Meehan's immediate reply was, 'I asked some months ago to be given a truth drug and to be interrogated under its influence.'

Lord Grant intervened, as he did quite often during this trial, 'Can't you tell the truth without having a truth drug, Meehan?'

The intonation, his expression, his failure to accord my client the common courtesy of Mr, as well as the inherent sarcasm, all played a part in his humiliation at that stage, and perhaps in the verdict of the jury.

Meehan recounted his movements in detail from Glasgow, Stranraer, Lochryanhall, Ballantrae, the Kilmarnock lay-by and back to Glasgow. Despite Stewart's perspicacity, he got little change out of Meehan. He scored one point, 'Do you know that your friend Griffiths had been guilty of such crimes as robbery with violence?'

This was below the belt and we objected. We pointed out that

Griffiths was a virtual co-accused, if one looked at the way the indictment had been framed (he had to be, to bring into account the car coat evidence), and that it was quite improper to bring out the criminal record of a co-accused during a trial, unless the latter decided to set up his own good character. This is a cherished principle of our criminal law.

The judge said that we had raised the question of Griffiths' character when we had brought out that he had stolen several cars and was being sought by the English police for this. The Crown, therefore, he said, was entitled to bring out his complete bad character. I thought, there's a world of a difference between stolen cars and being involved in robbery with violence.

'Continue,' said the judge to the Solicitor General. Come to think of it, I don't think that any one of Fairbairn's objections was upheld by the bench during this trial.

Another line put by the prosecution was that Meehan and Griffiths had gone to Stranraer (because it was incontrovertibly clear that they had) to set up an alibi in advance of the crime and that they had picked up the two girls so that they could later say, 'Who in their right minds would pick up strange girls in distress before or after committing such a crime?' I have heard of cunning planning, but this would have been of the super variety.

Meehan was also questioned, as I knew he would be, as to his reason for going to Stranraer in the first place. 'Was it to buy a car or to look over the Motor Taxation office with a view to later breaking in?' Meehan agreed that there were two reasons—the car and the Taxation Office—but they hadn't fancied the layout of the Taxation Office and had decided against it.

Asked about the paper in Griffiths' pocket, Meehan replied, 'Well, I can't answer for what was in Jim Griffiths' pocket.'

After four hours he left the witness box and returned to his seat in the dock. The cross-examination had been incisive, at times sarcastic—but always thoughtful and very well prepared.

Hours earlier Meehan had entered the witness box confident and cocky—he retired from it more than a little shaken and disconsolate, having suffered at the well-drilled hands of the Solicitor General and, to a lesser extent, those of the trial judge.

The moral of the story at this point is that even a truthful witness can be made to appear unsatisfactory at the hands of class, and class, undoubtedly, was what Ewan Stewart had. Having said all that, I felt that Meehan was a reasonable witness, although not as good as he thought he would have been.

I had intimated the names of Andrew Dick and John Skiverton, or Skivington (Big Skip), as defence witnesses, but they could not be traced, despite the efforts of sheriff officers.

Dramatically, we called Waddell after Meehan. This tactic had been decided by us earlier, in the event of the Crown not calling him. I knew the Crown would not take the risk of so doing and thus giving him immunity from prosecution.

Waddell took the oath—for whatever that meant—and was advised by Lord Grant that he did not require to answer any questions, the answers to which might incriminate him in the matter in issue, and that he did not enjoy immunity from prosecution.

Fairbairn handed him the piece of paper he had seen earlier, during the evidence of Ross.

Fairbairn—'During Ross's evidence you will remember we called you in so that Ross could hear your voice. The words on it were, 'Shut up, shut up, we'll send for an ambulance.' Fairbairn followed up, 'Have you ever said these words before this trial started?'

'I refuse to answer that question,' was the curt reply.

'Tell me this, then, have you ever heard anyone else say these words before I asked you to read them out two days ago?'

'No,' he said.

'You refuse to say whether you have ever used them before, do you?'

'Yes.'

Lord Grant intervened, 'Well, we must leave it there, Mr Fairbairn. No persuasion is allowed.'

Waddell was then asked about his movements before and after the crime. He said that he had gone to Carmichael's home with a carry-out of wine and whisky, 'round about midnight'. He didn't want to go home because he had been arguing with whoever he had been staying with at the time.

He would not give the name of the person he had been staying with. He was not even pressed by the judge to give this name.

He went on to say that he had stayed with Carmichael three or four times in the past. This had been contradicted by Carmichael in his earlier evidence. He went on to say that he had drunk with Carmichael on many occasions and at least 40 times since the year's start. Carmichael had said that he had met Waddell on only two or three occasions since December of 1968.

Waddell admitted that he was one of the first persons to be interviewed after the murder's discovery. When he was asked to report to the police station for a second interview his friend John Skiverton, or 'Big Skip' of the Club Bar, had taken him to see a solicitor by name of William Carlin.

Waddell was asked if he gave Carlin the princely sum of £200 to act for him and accompany him to the police station. I was pleasantly surprised when Waddell did not cut off Fairbairn by saying that he refused to reply, as was his entitlement. He admitted that Skiverton had taken him to Carlin's office.

Fairbairn asked, 'Did Skiverton give anything to Mr Carlin on that occasion?'

'I don't know.'

'Think carefully. Is it not the case that you gave Carlin the sum of £200?'

'No,' retorted Waddell.

He was now getting into deep water—later to cost him three years for perjury. He ought to have refused to answer—but perhaps his conscience had finally got through to him.

Fairbairn said, 'That's a lie' and 'We shall be calling Mr Carlin for the Defence.'

I had earlier taken a statement from Carlin who would say, I knew, that Waddell, and not Skiverton, had handed over the cash to him.

The judge again tried to rescue Waddell and, voice raised, rasped, 'Dealings between a solicitor and client are privileged.'

Fairbairn said Carlin would be called as his next witness.

'Only the client can waive the rule, not the solicitor,' said Lord Grant.

Our backs to the wall, Fairbairn asked Waddell, 'Are you willing that Mr Carlin should tell us whether or not you gave him any money on that occasion?'

I'll never know why Waddell did not say, 'I'm not answering that question.' This I fully expected to be his stance and an eminently sensible one at that . . .

Fairbairn—'Your evidence is that no money passed from you to Carlin on that occasion, when you went with Skiverton to his office?'

'Yes,' said Waddell.

Fairbairn—'I suggest you gave Carlin a substantial sum of money in five pound notes.'

The judge, clearly worried, explained to Waddell that his dealings with solicitors were private and confidential, he could refuse to answer the question if he wished.

A nod is as good as a wink, they say, but to my astonishment Waddell could have seen neither. He replied, 'I will answer it, I never gave him any money.'

He had now committed himself fully, as well as giving us a lifeline. He went on to deny ever meeting McIntyre in Dick's house. He further denied ever speaking to McCafferty in Barlinnie. Waddell was probably the worst witness called in the conduct of this case—at least, that was my view.

Bill Carlin was called next by us. Fairbairn said, 'In the course of your business, did a man Ian Waddell come to you in July of this year?'

'That is so, yes,' was the reply. Carlin continued: 'He was brought to my office by another client of mine, John Skiverton. [*I must have lost Skiverton as a client somewhere along the line.*] He introduced me to him and said that the Glasgow CID wished to question him in connection with the Ayr murder.' Carlin said he then rang the CID and told them of Waddell's presence in his office. Later he went in with him.

Fairbairn—'Did Waddell give you money?'

'Yes, he did, and Skiverton said that if I were to act for him, he (Waddell) better pay me. Waddell gave me £200,' said Carlin. 'In twenty pound notes.'

'Did this surprise you?' said Fairbairn.

'Yes, to a certain extent it did,' replied Carlin.

Carlin went on to say that Waddell wanted him to act if he were charged with the murder.
So the possibility was clearly in his mind . . . .
Carlin continued that he had never been asked to return this amount or any part of it.

Other witnesses of moment were McIntyre and McCafferty.

McIntyre said that he had been approached by Andrew Dick to join Waddell and him at a robbery in Ayr. He went on to say that he had bought a car in Ballachulish and had altered its colour. He then met Waddell in Dick's house and heard about the fact that it was to be a 'tie-up job' involving old people. He withdrew from the scheme at this stage.

Fairbairn tried to bring out what Waddell had told McIntyre, but this line was objected to by both Ewan Stewart and Lord Grant. The trial judge then said to Fairbairn, 'Mr Fairbairn, would you please not be more stupid than you really are.' Yes, compliments were flying throughout the court that day!

Robert McCafferty, another prisoner, followed and said that he had spoken to Waddell on exercise in Barlinnie, when Waddell had told him that he had done the Ayr job and that Meehan was quite innocent. He went on to say that Waddell said, 'What can I do if the police make a mess of it?' Waddell had then gone on to say that the man with him on the raid had telephoned, but only to the exchange operator—'Otherwise, there would have been no murder at all.'

The manager of the Lochryanhall Hotel, Cairnryan, and a fair number of alibi witnesses sought out by me, were called, with limited 'cross' by Stewart. Members of Meehan's family gave evidence on his behalf. The defence case was then closed and I awaited the speeches anxiously.

Stewart spoke first next day and stressed the various points in the Crown case. 'The strands are there,' he said. He then went out of his way to damn Fairbairn with faint praise. He said, 'I need not remind you that Fairbairn, who will follow me, has already made his name as one of the foremost of defence counsel.' He reminded them of his astonishing record (confident that there would be no interruption from the bench) of successes, and the fact that many juries in the past had been influenced by his 'silver tongue and sharp mind'. He warned them that Fairbairn's speech would be brilliant, but admonished that they should not be too overawed or taken in by his high standard of advocacy. 'He is always at his persuasive best, irrespective of the type of person he represents. He will, I am certain, give you good reasons for acquitting Meehan.'

Stewart was making the very best of what seemed to me to be a loose and unconvincing Crown case. 'Meehan is a cunning fox,' he said. 'He ensured that he was identifiable all over Stranraer on the night of 5 July.'

At this stage he seemed to accept the major part of our alibi—it was so good. He said that our special defences of alibi and impeachment were lodged merely as a diversionary tactic to try to deflect the Jury's attention from the salient facts. 'Defence tactics and clever ones at that,' he volunteered.

He finished by highlighting the evidence of 'Pat' and 'Jim', the voice identification by Ross, the fact that Meehan had the opportunity, due to his own statement, and the telltale pieces of paper in the car-coat pocket.

Fairbairn followed, much of his thunder having been stolen in advance by the shrewd, determined prosecutor. He went on to say, wisely, that if Griffiths—a man who had clear and ready access to firearms, as we now knew—had been involved in the robbery then wouldn't he have taken a weapon or weapons to Blackburn Place and so force Ross to give details of the safe keys? 'After all, you can't argue with a gun.' He went on to say that this method would have been much more expeditious.

Fairbairn summarised the defence case succinctly and, in my opinion, gave one of his finest ever jury addresses—and I have heard him on many an occasion. After finishing, he returned to our table, rather spent, and I said to him, 'You've never been better.'

I now awaited the charge from the judge—so much would depend on this.

In the course of the few days' evidence I had said to Fairbairn on occasions that the judge's approach seemed to be biased in favour of the Crown. Fairbairn agreed, but said, 'Don't worry, his charges are always fair and down the middle.'

After Fairbairn's closing speech I thought that we had 'stolen' a Not Proven verdict. Had this been the case then the matter would have been a seven-day wonder, as opposed to the epoch-making saga which was to last 15 years. Had the verdict been one of acquittal I would have been delighted—spared many years of anguish, worry, heartbreak, and acute frustration.

Lord Grant charged the jury at length. At the outset he told them, fairly, to disregard the frightening events at Holyrood Crescent which climaxed with the shooting of Jim Griffiths. 'Put those events out of your minds,' he said—at the same time underlining them. 'Meehan's position should not be prejudiced as a result of the conduct of Griffiths on 15 July.' At this stage of the charge I was happy enough.

He then rehearsed most of the evidence and pointed out that it was, in the main, of a circumstantial nature. 'Circumstantial evidence, however, can be very strong and is sometimes preferable to direct evidence. You must look at the cumulative effect—link by link—before deciding on whether or not the Prosecution has proved its case beyond reasonable doubt and to the necessary high standard required by our law.' He added, to my displeasure, 'It is easy enough to demolish each item like a ninepin—a natural common defence tactic and a perfectly legitimate one. The cumulative effect is of lasting importance.'

He went on to stress that Meehan had been charged acting along with Griffiths and that when two persons embark on a criminal enterprise the law holds both equally responsible.

He mentioned the tiny pieces of paper allegedly found in the car coat and underlined the significance of this—as if we didn't know already.

He then dealt with our special defence of impeachment of Waddell and Phillips (we had not proceeded with the Phillips one) and, to my amazement, the judge withdrew from the jury's consideration our defence of impeachment of Waddell. I shall quote him as accurately as the certified shorthand notes allow: 'The defence of impeachment or incrimination has not been established in this case—indeed, there is not even remotely sufficient evidence to establish it—you would not be entitled to hold it established. There is no evidence which even remotely suggests that Ian Waddell and Samuel Phillips were the perpetrators of this ghastly crime.'

With the Phillips aspect I entirely agreed as we had not pursued this line at the trial.

The judge went on to say:

'Evidence had been led that Waddell made certain statements incriminating himself. He, however, in the box, denied having made these statements. Even if you accept the evidence that he did make those statements, that would not entitle you to hold, even on a balance of probabilities, that he was one of the perpetrators.

'As I think I made clear to you yesterday, the evidence that a witness made a particular statement, which, in the witness box, he denies having made, may be used for the purely negative purpose of destroying that witness's credibility, ensuring that his evidence is untrue.

'It is, however, of no value in establishing positively that what was said in the statement is true. There must be positive evidence of that, although, of course, that may be more readily received if what I might call the opposing witness has been shown to be a liar.

'In the present case, there is wholly insufficient evidence, even on a balance of probabilities, as I have said, that Waddell was one of the perpetrators.

'So there is no evidence in law on which you could find a special defence of impeachment or incrimination established.'

In my opinion this is an incorrect statement of the law. By impeaching Waddell we had put him in the dock. That being so, anything of an

*incriminating nature said by him was, and must be, evidence against him.
Statements made by an accused to prisoners, whilst awaiting trial, can be led
against him. Frequently, statements made to fellow prisoners within the
police station are led in evidence by officers who happen to overhear them. I
repeat—by impeaching Waddell we had put him in the same position as an
accused person, for the duration of the trial.*

My stomach muscles tightened when he said that—I thought he
was indicating to the jury that they should convict ... perhaps he
was.

True to form, Lord Grant did not dwell on the fact that Ross had
said that the two raiders had Scottish, indeed Glasgow, accents. That,
after all, was one of our best points.

He went on to remind the jury that Ross had said that the raiders
had taken whisky and lemonade, 'and it turned out that Meehan does
drink whisky and lemonade'. He had the grace to say that 'that does
not get you very far'—but he said it nonetheless.

He finished his not-too-favourable jury charge by defining the
meaning of reasonable doubt and culpable homicide. The jury retired
for what seemed to be an eternity—in fact, barely two hours.

During the retirement I reminded Fairbairn of his prediction about
the judge's charge to the jury. He had told me that whereas his
conduct seemed unfavourable to the accused in his view—that's
Fairbairn's view—the charge would be straight and down the middle.
This it certainly was not.

12

During the time of the jury's retirement I was extremely ill at ease and paced up and down the beautiful front hallway at Parliament Square, looking at, but not seeing, the numerous excellent paintings and sculptures of illustrious legal luminaries of bygone eras.

I remember the Solicitor General's assistant, John McCluskey, approaching me and telling me not to be over-anxious. He felt, he said, that it would be a Not Proven verdict. This statement from an opponent helped to alleviate my anguish and how I hoped that he would be right. I knew within myself that in the event of a conviction the matter would never be allowed to rest there. I envisaged a tortuous period for me if the verdict went against us, and knew that our appeal prospects would not be good, such was the feeling about my client.

To pass some of the time I went downstairs to see Meehan during the recess. He was despondent and felt that, innocent as he was, he was on the verge of being convicted. I tried to inculcate a measure of confidence into him but realised that I was not convincing. Our half-smoked cigarettes littered the stone floor.

The jury returned and I studied them intently. The thought of conviction appalled me, because this saga would be on-going. Many of the jurors turned their heads away from the dock, although Meehan's eyes were riveted on them.

The foreman said, 'Guilty by majority.'

The judge, never missing a trick, commented on the deplorable record of Meehan and duly sentenced him to life imprisonment.

Meehan stood firmly to attention, looked at the judge and said, 'I want to say this, sir—I'm innocent of this crime and so is Jim Griffiths.' Looking at the jury, he said, 'You have made a terrible mistake.'

This was one of the rare occasions in my considerable experience when an accused person has seen fit to speak from the dock immediately after being sentenced to life imprisonment. I will never forget his words, or his state of helplessness.

Fairbairn, Smith and I went down to see him in the cells—a prospect I did not relish. I saw, clearly, the tears in his eyes. Perhaps he saw mine, too, when he said, 'How could this happen? How can a jury convict an innocent man of a crime so heinous?'

I told him how sorry I was and that an appeal would be considered. I said that I would go over the judge's charge with a fine toothcomb that very night. I was extremely unhappy about the way in which the defence of impeachment had been dramatically discarded, or jettisoned, by the judge.

All three of us did our best to comfort this distraught man. We talked about the appeal but I knew that Meehan, sensible as he was, would not hold out much by way of hope at that forum.

In despair, I made the apparently lengthy journey back to Glasgow. I knew that there never had been a Royal Pardon in Scotland for matters of such a nature. (*The first was to be six years later, 1975, in the case of Maurice Swanson, who had been wrongly convicted of bank robbery.*)

And so an epic struggle was to start—at times the ultimate goal (Meehan's vindication) was merely the sometimes flickering, though tiny, shaft of light at the end of a seemingly endless tunnel of stark, uninterrupted darkness.

When I returned to Glasgow I was interviewed by David Scott of BBC television. I remember saying—and this was brave of me because solicitors had never publicly commented adversely on a murder conviction before—'Although my client was today convicted of the Ayr murder this is not the end of the matter. In my view, there has been a miscarriage of justice in this case. Eventually, I pray, justice will be done. I know I am right.'

I worried about repercussions—but there were none. I arranged a consultation with Fairbairn and Smith, to go into the matter of the appeal.

Next, David Scott phoned me to say that the BBC had a tape relating to Griffiths, following upon an interview with him at Gartree

JB outside the Ross bungalow

ord Grant (trial judge) (Courtesy of The Scotsman)

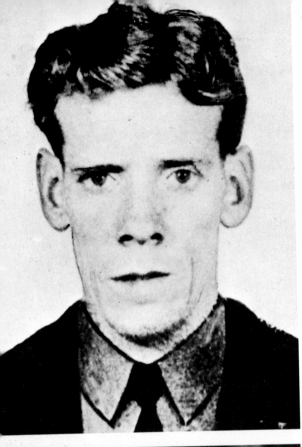

William 'Tank' McGuinness (Courtesy of the *Evening Tir*

Ian Waddell (Courtesy of the *Evening Times*)

The 'Free PM Committee': JB, J. Ross Harper, Burnside, Kennedy and Murray (Courtesy of The Scotsman)

JB and John (Gypsy) Winning (on the day of his acquittal)
(Courtesy of the *Scottish Daily Express*)

Lord Cameron (Courtesy of *The Scotsman*)

Elizabeth R

ELIZABETH THE SECOND, by the Grace of God
of the United Kingdom of Great Britain
and Northern Ireland and of Our other
Realms and Territories QUEEN, Head of the
Commonwealth, Defender of the Faith, to
all to whom these Presents shall come,
GREETING!

WHEREAS Patrick Connolly Meehan was at the High Court holden
at Edinburgh on the twenty-fourth day of October 1969 convicted of
murder and sentenced to life imprisonment;

NOW KNOW YE that We in consideration of some circumstances
humbly represented unto Us and of Our Prerogative Royal, Proper
Motion, and Royal Clemency are graciously pleased to extend Our
Grace and Mercy to the said Patrick Connolly Meehan and to grant
him Our Free Pardon in respect of the said conviction thereby
pardoning, remitting and releasing unto him all pains, penalties
and punishments whatsoever that from the said conviction may come.

Given at Our Court at *St James*
the *19th* day of *May* 1976
in the Twenty-fifth Year of Our
Reign.

BY HER MAJESTY'S COMMAND
(SIGNED) *BRUCE MILLAN*

CERTIFIED A TRUE COPY

The Royal Pardon superscribed by the Queen (Courtesy of Raymond Beltrami, the Evening Times)

The Queen and I (Courtesy of Malky McCormick)

At long last! Meehan signs—on the dotted line—for his compensation (Courtesy of the Glasgow Herald)

D.A.O. EDWARD, 32, HERIOT ROW, EDINBURGH EH3 6ES. 031-225 7153

13/2/84.

Dear Mr Beltrami,

A rather belated note to thank you for your letter of 2nd Feb. It was reassuring to receive, on the same day, letters of thanks from the Secretary of State, your client and yourself!

Yours sincerely,

David Edward

The note from the D.A.O. Edward Q.C., Assessor

Left: Mr Joseph Beltrami,
Right: Mr Nicholas Fairbairn,

JB and Fairbairn (John Smith's window in Glasgow at launching of Kennedy's book) (Courtesy of Raymond Beltrami)

Author at his desk (Courtesy of the Daily Record)

Prison. The significance was obvious and I obtained the tape and lodged it with the justiciary as new evidence—evidence which had been unavailable and unknown to me prior to the trial.

I lodged this all-revealing tape [which the BBC in London were kind enough to give me] for the abortive and futile appeal.

The three senior judges constituting the Court of Criminal Appeal in Edinburgh and the man in the chair in particular, Lord Justice General Clyde, leaned forward and said to us, Nicholas Fairbairn, John Smith and myself: 'You've already had one trial, how many trials do you want—half a dozen?'

The crucial tape, as I maintain it was, was never heard by our appeal court. Indeed, it took all of 50 minutes to dispose of our ten grounds of appeal.

It was pointed out that the trial judge, Lord Justice Clerk Grant, had advised the jury in his charge to disregard entirely the fact that Griffiths virtually committed suicide on 15 July 1969, rather than await his arrest.

This, indeed, was true but I often wondered why the Crown deemed it necessary to lead this graphic evidence in the first place, if it were not relevant to the trial of Meehan. Had this not been done, it would then have been unnecessary for the judge to ask the jury, the masters of fact, to expunge it from their deliberations for fear of prejudice to the accused.

Abraham Ross had stated unequivocally that both assailants had Glasgow accents. Now, Ross had been born and brought up in Glasgow and still had business interests there. One would surely think that he would be the first to appreciate and distinguish such an accent from England's North Lancashire, where Griffiths' Rochdale is. It was important to be able to demonstrate the deceased's normal spoken voice, as one could in the tape. There was no way, and I heard the tape on at least six occasions, that Griffiths's voice and accent could possibly be described as 'Glasgow'.

Oh, had only the jury the benefit of this at the time! True it was brought out at the trial that Griffiths did not have such an accent—that was one of our long suits—but actually to have heard him speak would have brought much more emphasis and force to the point.

Secondly, the main drift of the recorded interview was that Griffiths, then on the verge of freedom, stated that he would never be back in prison—he had had enough.

Frankly, I did not expect success at the Appeal Court, although it could have been conducted with more dignity. The Appeal was over—ignominiously dismissed—and I wondered where I should turn next. I had a number of names: Skiverton, Waddell, Dick, Carmichael and Mrs Carmichael—all of whom knew a lot, but my next move escaped me for the moment.

I went to the prison to let Meehan see that he had not been dropped. I saw him in the normal interview room, this time in the presence of a prison warder. I asked the warder to leave us, as I wished to discuss private and confidential matters with my client. He replied, 'I have strict orders to remain in the room and listen to everything that is said.'

I flushed with rage and said, 'This is highly irregular and improper. No one has the right to give such an order.' This had never happened to me before and I had been interviewing prisoners there for some 13 years, at that time. 'What's so special about this case?' I barked at the poor dutiful warder who was only obeying orders. I was about to storm off to the Governor when Meehan restrained me saying, 'It doesn't matter, we have nothing to hide. Whatever he reports back can only be to our good.'

That was to be the first and only time that I was to interview a prisoner with a warder present in the room.

By now the action-packed year of 1969 had passed on and 1970 had dawned. I was totally at a loss with regard to my next move. I continually reassured myself by thinking, as did Mr Micawber, that something must surely turn up—but what? When? It was impossible to abandon my normal business—the mortgage had to be paid, matters required to proceed, no matter how mundane they appeared to be, despite the trauma of Meehan's conviction. There were occasions when I felt like requesting leave of absence from the office—say one month—but the pressures were such that this was wholly unrealistic, and impractical.

However, certain Crown witnesses were re-interviewed in the passage of time. In particular, the 'stand-ins' at the identification parades, as well as the witnesses from the lay-by, Burns and Smith. I well remember travelling to Kilmarnock to speak to Burns and Smith, who went over all the circumstances of the parade with me, then caused me to form the view that Ross had been last, and not first, at the parade. Then Burns phoned me two days later to tell me that the police had found out that I had seen her and she asked me not to see her again. I formed the view, and still do, that my home and office telephones had been 'bugged'. Irene had been told by the police not to see me again. Why? After all, the Appeal had been dismissed two months earlier.

Then there was the first of interminable 'breakthroughs' in this troublesome case. After the conviction I had written a dossier to the

Crown office, pointing out the apparent act of perjury by Waddell who had blatantly contradicted Carlin when stating that he had not given any money to the lawyer.

Shortly after this, Waddell appeared at Edinburgh Sheriff Court, charged with perjury at Meehan's trial. Matters were now moving at last. This development excited me, in that the powers of the Crown were prepared to act against one of their own witnesses—although I wondered what else they could do in the circumstances. Waddell had been so stupid in not taking 'the Fifth'. And, after all, we had impeached Waddell at Meehan's trial—even although the trial judge had seen fit to withdraw the matter, off his own bat, and without a 'by your leave'.

Three weeks later, Waddell appeared at Edinburgh High Court before Lord Cameron and pleaded guilty to the charge of perjury. He was sentenced to three years' imprisonment and Lord Cameron told him, 'Had you not lied to the jury, they might have taken a very different view of an unemployed labourer handing over a substantial sum of money to a solicitor.'

I felt that Lord Cameron had spoken advisedly, and that this must be a signal to re-open Meehan's case.

A second dossier was sent to the Scottish Secretary, Willie Ross, suggesting that Meehan's case should now be reviewed, particularly in view of the fact that Waddell had openly and publicly admitted to perjury at the trial of Meehan. I quoted the remarks of Lord Cameron and said, 'This man was an extremely important witness at the trial and the jury's view (at least the majority of them) might have been altered had they realised that he had not told the complete truth.'

Alas, there was no reaction whatsoever to my dossier. I knew that much more would require to be done to cause the authorities to reflect.

I said earlier that I considered that my own phone had been bugged. After the 1976 Pardon I phoned Meehan on many occasions about one thing or another. We had a standing joke. I would phone and Meehan would say, 'Say nothing until you hear the click.' Lo and behold, there would be a click and we would then converse. There was no doubt in my mind that Meehan's phone was bugged as from 1976.

Having despatched my two dossiers, I was the first to appreciate that matters would never be as easy as that! The establishment was not for budging. Then Meehan wrote to me—how well I came to recognise his scrawly hand:

Dear Mr Beltrami, I have spoken to Andrew Dick and he says he
will come clean about everything. He confirms everything McIntyre
said. He is very worried that he might be charged with receiving
money from the Ayr crime. It was part of this that he gave to Mc-
Intyre.

On 6 July in the morning Waddell came to Dick's house along
with Donald Carmichael between 11 a.m. and midday. Dick asked
Waddell what had kept him and Waddell said he was over at
Carmichael's house fixing up his alibi, and he had to keep Carmichael
sweet!

Dick is also saying that Carmichael put up a false alibi for Waddell.
He said that the police did not look very hard for him to serve a
Citation, as the factor knew where he had moved to, and his children
were still at the same school.

I can well imagine that the police would not look too hard for Dick.
Dick also says that when Waddell gave him the £100 on the morning
of Sunday 6 July, he remarked, 'We got a nice turn.' Carmichael was
there at the time.

My immediate reaction had been that Dick had been slow in telling us
this—how easy it is after the trial, and how late.

I next had the first of a number of meetings with the late Frank
McElhone, Labour MP for the Gorbals. He was extremely receptive
and agreed to travel with Fairbairn and me to Peterhead where
Meehan now was. John Smith, of his own volition, had disappeared
from the picture. Fairbairn was soon to disappear virtually as well. To
be frank, there were times when I wished that I would be allowed to
disappear, too. . . .

When the three of us saw Meehan in Peterhead we found him to be
sulky, difficult and resentful. We could understand that. Not much
came out of this meeting, but it did indicate to Meehan that we were
still very much on his side, that he had not been abandoned.

I felt that up to this time Waddell's position was reasonably clear—he
had been involved. But what of this ubiquitous second man? Up to this
point, there had been maintained a wall of silence so far as his identity
was concerned. Prior to the trial I had been misled into thinking that G.
McCawley, Samuel Phillips, and others, had been 'the second man'.

After a few months I decided to see John Skivington or Skiverton, a
man who had failed to answer his citation at Meehan's trial. I made
enquires as to his whereabouts. This was yet another occasion when I
went to the underworld.

Nothing, of course, had happened to Skiverton, despite his failure to appear at a High Court trial. Indeed, one felt that he'd almost been encouraged, along with Andrew Dick, to 'fail to trap'. I was told that Skiverton was managing a run-down, working-class pub in a row of stark, grey tenements in a seedy area of Springburn.

Skiverton, as I remembered him from his last jury trial, was powerfully built and of average height. He was then in his early forties, slightly greying, and someone who looked capable of acquitting himself well in the square ring.

I decided to see him at once, as I knew he was quite knowledgeable about the esoteric facts of this murder case. Intentionally, I arrived at the bleak public house just on the dot of what was then opening time, 5 p.m., and, on entering, I saw that the place had no customers and that Skiverton was behind the bar. I approached him—he recognised me, of course—and told him that I would like to talk to him in private. He ushered me into a small room on the right-hand side of the public bar.

I told him why I was there—clearly he knew, in any event—and said that I was extremely concerned about Meehan's conviction. I told him that I thought he could assist me in connection with the clarification of the whole matter.

At once, after this preamble, I asked him for the identity of the second man in the Ayr murder. I told him that I had been given the names of McCawley and Phillips but that this was clearly wrong information.

He thought for only some ten seconds and I wondered if he would ask me to leave. Looking at me positively, he said, somewhat cryptically, 'The second man is a client of yours and he has a nickname.' This was, indeed, a challenge to me. Taken aback more than somewhat at the suddenness and definite nature of Skiverton's statement, I went over one or two nicknames of some clients—without an iota of response from Skiverton.

Minutes later, I hit the jackpot. I said, 'Tank McGuinness.'

Skiverton looked at me firmly and his expression was a clear indication that I had been spot-on. He merely said, 'You're on the right track.' But he went on to say, 'You know that I will deny that this conversation ever took place.'

I thanked him and left the premises without even buying a drink. I had been there for about 15 minutes, but was satisfied that 'Tank' had almost certainly been involved. I could not see Skiverton using the name of this psychopath called 'Tank' as a diversion. I remembered also one of the letters from Barlinnie in which the name McGuinness had been dropped by McCusker. One simply didn't use the name of 'Tank' McGuinness loosely.

Driving back to my office, I wondered as to the reliability of Skiverton. I did not think that he would mislead me in this regard—he had no previous notice of my appearance—although others had, prior to the trial.

I weighed up the new development. I knew that 'Tank' was a violent psychopath and that he was feared by most criminals, although so small and slight in build. I began to understand the reason for the wall of silence which had confronted me up to that memorable day.

I could not, of course, communicate with McGuinness—this would have been most improper. It would have to come from him, as it did the day he was liberated from Barlinnie after the dropping of the murder charge in the case of Richards. I hoped—and that's all I could do at this stage—that 'Tank' would contact me about the matter at some future date. But I was not over-confident in this regard.

The upshot was that I became more frustrated that ever. What would happen next? I asked myself.

Strangely enough, the only occasion I did not represent 'Tank' McGuinness, my client for all of 15 years, was in late 1970, when he was charged with theft of jewellery at, of all places, Ayr High Court. There were four other accused and I represented one, Zack Williamson. I wondered at that time why 'Tank' had seen fit to instruct another lawyer, the late Bill Dunlop, but thought that the reason was simply that I was acting for someone else in the same case.

In this case the only one to be convicted was 'Tank' [for reset only] and he was given three years' imprisonment. In January 1971, the conviction against 'Tank' was quashed because the judge had told the jury, 'Scrutinise carefully, as a matter of law, the evidence of the accused, McGuinness.' There should, of course, be no such strictures on an accused's evidence.

I now think that he failed to instruct me because the Meehan case was particularly 'hot' at this time. There had been a lot of activity duly reported in the Press and television. I was upset at not being instructed by 'Tank'—I had had good results for him on a number of occasions before that and after, for that matter. One does not like loosing a good client, even temporarily. One's pride is affected.

13

Over the years 1970–75 I received a number of anonymous letters about the case. Without exception, they supported Meehan's innocence and some gave me points of assistance.

I formed the view that one of the letters had been written by someone in the CID, who had a considerable knowledge of police work. This letter told me, among other things, that at the parade on 14 July 1969 Meehan was wearing a serpent ring on his left ring-finger. It went on to say that this ring was easily identifiable.

These letters were not of great assistance to me at the end of the day, but they did indicate the number of members of the public who felt, as I did, that the result of the trial had been disturbing.

I travelled to Peterhead again to see Meehan. I wanted to give him this new line of hope. He was surly and extremely sarcastic. He had turned against me, as if it had been my fault. His demeanour, I suppose, was to be expected—he was innocent, after all. I remember saying to him, annoyed at his attitude, 'After all, if the jury had believed you, you would not be here.' I was trying to put across to him that there had been some blame, if one could call it that, attached to him.

On the drive back from Peterhead I thought about the next move and the possibility of trying to arrange an adjournment debate in Parliament. I consulted Frank McElhone MP. Frank agreed to write to the Crown Office, Scottish Secretary and Lord Advocate. This met with no success whatsoever.

In the meantime, Meehan's son, Patrick, was becoming fairly active on his father's behalf. He interviewed a number of the parade witnesses.

Meehan at this time, unhappy with me, wrote to other lawyers—Ross Harper and Len Murray. He must have thought—and who could blame him?—that three heads were better than one. I met both Harper and Murray, who knew precious little about the case. There was no way that they could help me piece together the fantastic jigsaw.

In 1972 there was the further development mentioned earlier, the arrest of McGuinness and another in the murder of the man Richards in Sandaig Road, Barlannark.

At about this time Meehan wrote to Ludovic Kennedy, outlining his plight and asking him to intervene on his behalf. Within days 'Ludo' came to my office by appointment and spent several hours with me. His intention was to clear the 'monstrous injustice of Meehan's case'. He was assured of my full co-operation in a partnership that was to pay substantial dividends in the years to come.

Ludo and I 'gelled' from our first meeting. An outsider might have said that one complemented the other, to the undoubted advantage of Meehan. Even at this stage, matters could not be described as rosy or even hopeful. Had there been a light at the end of the tunnel, it certainly was not being detected by me!

In the meantime, Meehan had gone into solitary confinement in Peterhead. He claimed that he should not be in prison in the first place and was not liable for prison chores.

Ludo's application impressed me profoundly—he was quick to bring himself up to date with matters. At another meeting with Ludo he told me that he was launching a 'Free Paddy Meehan Committee'. The first meeting, he said, would take place in Edinburgh—at The North British Hotel—on a Sunday afternoon. I agreed to join the committee, along with Ross Harper, Len Murray, David Scott, now of Scottish Television, David Burnside, Bert Kerrigan, an advocate and a reporter from the *Sunday Times*. This reporter was a close friend of Ludovic.

There was great media interest, no doubt due to the involvement of Ludovic Kennedy. The North British was crowded at our first meeting—Press from everywhere in the country, in the knowledge that we were challenging, publicly, the High Court jury's verdict, not to mention that the matter had already been ventilated in the final Court of Criminal Appeal. (It should be noted that in Scotland there is no right of appeal to the House of Lords.) Ludo was elected Chairman of the Committee, which was to go on from strength to strength.

In the early summer of 1972, Waddell, now released after his perjury sentence, was arrested again, this time on a charge of being in possession of a loaded revolver, and of a breach of the peace. Waddell nominated as his solicitor William Dunn, a partner of mine at that time. Waddell decided to plead guilty to the serious charge.

When the date of the court appearance came round, Mr Dunn was on holiday. I went to see Waddell in the cells prior to the hearing. He very clearly knew me, although I had never spoken to him before and when I explained the position vis-à-vis my partner, I asked him if he wished me to have the matter adjourned on his behalf. He said, no, he would like the case disposed of at once. I reminded him, as if it were necessary, of my involvement with Meehan and asked him if he wished me to act notwithstanding that. Waddell, said, 'Yes, go ahead.' I then took his instructions in connection with the charge of being in possession of a loaded revolver with intent to endanger life.

I spoke up for Waddell, resulting in a lenient sentence from Sheriff Pirie—12 months' imprisonment, backdated to 4 June, the time of his arrest. The minor charge of breach of the peace had been dropped by the Crown.

Now, before that, there had been no mention of Meehan's case by either of us. Later that morning one of the court police officers told me that Waddell wished to see me. I rushed upstairs, pleased to know that the request came from him. I saw him in the small bare consulting room. He was clearly delighted at the result of his case and had expected a remit to the High Court, with which he was so familiar.

'No appeal,' he volunteered. Waddell went on to say that he now wished to help Meehan.

'In what way?' I invited.

Waddell said that he had calculated that his own release date would be early February 1973. 'I am agreeable to be questioned under the truth drug on that date at the BBC studios and the whole matter should be televised.' He went on to say that he would not be doing this for money. This pleased me, as money would be the point that the many doubters would latch on to.

He asked me to advise the Press of the experiment. I was excited and told him that I would discuss the whole matter with him in Barlinnie in the near future.

I said, 'Supposing you say nothing of moment whilst under the drug, how will that help Meehan?'

He replied simply, 'I can help him.'

I then put to Waddell the question I had wanted to ask him for years. 'Is Meehan innocent of the Ayr murder?'

Waddell looked through me with his grey eyes, and said, 'What do you think?' He had put the ball back in my court and had not reinforced my confidence.

I thought to myself, 'What sort of reply was that?'—it was equivocal and unsatisfactory. I did not pursue the matter further at that stage.

But the whole prospect excited me. I saw Waddell on several occasions in Barlinnie Prison, telling him that if he demanded money the authorities would claim that it had been purely a commercial venture. He told me that there would be no financial involvement. Again, that pleased me.

Later, unfortunately, Waddell changed his mind in this regard and told me that he had given the matter a lot of thought. He required a substantial sum of money because he would be hounded by the CID and would be obliged to leave Scotland. He would require, he said, to start a new life in England. He asked me to negotiate with BBC television, which I did. I contacted my friend David Scott who had always shown an interest in the case. I was disappointed at the change of stance by Waddell and would have been much happier had there been no cash inducement. At the same time, he did have a point.

Shortly before his February release I told Waddell that I could not continue to act for him because of my concern for Meehan. He understood fully and asked me to contact another solicitor, by name of Robert Gibson, of Ingram Street, Glasgow. I was quite pleased to do this because I knew Gibson quite well. He was a man of ability and considerable experience. I duly contacted him.

I felt that I would be vulnerable and open to criticism if I continued to act for Waddell. One cannot, or should not, be seen to wear two hats.

The gangling Waddell was no fool and had sly animal cunning, despite his handling of the Carlin episode in the witness box. He mentioned to me that as the court had held that Meehan's application for examination under the truth drug was incompetent, the Court could not go along with anything he might say under its influence. In short, he could not lose. Before I brought in Gibson, Waddell made it clear to me that under the drug he would say a great deal and this must be to Meehan's advantage.

On 2 February 1973 at 6.45 a.m. BBC reporters David Scott and Ken Vass met Waddell on his release from Barlinnie Prison. Scott had a minuscule tape recorder secreted in his tie—and an interesting conversation took place.

I had, of course, told David Scott of Waddell's wish for £20,000. Both of us knew that BBC TV would not pay that sum—possibly £100 at most. However, it was decided by us to string Waddell along and try to get him talking. Perhaps this may seem to have been unfair, but we were playing for high stakes and dealing with, after all, a murderer.

In the car Scott asked Waddell what he had to say about the Ayr murder, to which Waddell replied, 'I'll need to see my lawyer Gibson.' He went on to say that the only question he did not wish to be asked under the drug was who his accomplice was. He said that he would answer every other question about the murder.

Waddell agreed to another meeting that same day to discuss further details—at Gibson's Ingram Street office. Kennedy, Scott, Vass and I duly turned up—but there was no Waddell. He was drunk.

A day or two later Waddell was traced by Scott and Vass, complete with tape recorder. Waddell stated that he wanted £20,000 to do the experiment, 'so that I can leave the country before I'm assassinated'. He went on to tell them that he would establish Meehan's innocence. He admitted that the names Pat and Jim had been used during the robbery but not to incriminate Meehan and Griffiths. 'I didn't even know them.' He gave details of the bungalow never yet disclosed.

Unlike the laconic 'Tank', Waddell was a loud-mouth. For years he had been a petty criminal and only within recent times was emerging into the big time, which he dearly loved. He was six feet in height, fairly slim in build, rough features, very often with several days of growth, reddish hair and a slight speech impediment. And had he not stumbled over the word 'ambulance' while giving his recitation at Meehan's trial?

Waddell told them, all on tape, that £3,500 had been taken and that his Carmichael alibi had been false. He went on to say that he had never met Meehan before the crime, although he had heard of him. He had never heard of Griffiths.

'A ladder,' he said, 'was used to cut the telephone wires. I had done the murder—me and the other chap tied them up. I still maintain that she wasn't murdered—not intentionally, I mean.'

On being asked by Scott as to why he now wished to confess, he replied, 'I feel sorry for the bloke. It canna' be a mistake—Meehan has been framed.'

Asked if he was not afraid of being charged himself, he said, 'The evidence they need to use against me would, under this drug, be illegal, as far as I know.'

That same day Scott and Vass went to see Gibson who told them that if the experiment was successful and Waddell helped Meehan, then the price was to be £30,000. If Waddell said nothing of moment then he would expect nothing in return.

Gibson, and Waddell for that matter, were unaware that two vital conversations had already been taped. So far as Gibson was concerned, no decision was made on the figure now required. In fact, the BBC had already made its decision.

Meanwhile, in yet another letter from Peterhead, Meehan said, 'The Ross family was hostile to you and they have been told that you were a fly man.' He said that Ross had been told not to let me pull the wool over their eyes.

On reading the letter I recalled that when I arranged to precognosce Ross before the trial, his brother-in-law, a Glasgow solicitor, had insisted that I do it in his office and in his presence. This struck me as being odd at the time, but I was anxious to see Ross personally and had to make this concession. Yes, I recall that it had been a very difficult precognition. It was like drawing teeth.

The letter went on to say that Ross had been told that the truth drug publicity was a gimmick and that there had never been a 'hope in hell' of its being allowed. He asked me not to make any further enquiries from the Ross family because of their hostility towards me. He would engage an enquiry agent through his wife. Thus the surprising letter ended.

Shortly after this, and in desperation, I wrote to the Clerk of Justiciary in Edinburgh to request the names of the jury members as I wished to interview them. I received back a sharp slap on the wrist and was told of the impropriety of such a suggestion. In Scotland, so far, there have been no instances of lawyers conferring with jurors *after* a case has ended. I had also written to the Scottish Office, yet once more, requesting that they send an official, knowledgeable in the case, to interview Meehan in Peterhead. I had been there on a number of occasions and often wished that someone on the other side could have been present to listen to him. The whole ambience of the interview room reeked with the pathetic situation of a man clearly innocent, but just as surely doomed. But they would not send anyone to see him and assess his protestations. Those were occasions when I felt no one else wanted to know—that the boat was not to be allowed to be rocked.

One thing that always puzzled me about Ian Waddell was how on earth he managed to team up with a professional like 'Tank'. I always thought that 'Tank' would be more discreet and judicious in his choice of associate. It emerged later that McGuinness had been brought into the scheme at the eleventh hour, so to speak.

I had never heard of Waddell before 1969—he was never in the McGuinness range. At Meehan's trial Waddell was unimpressive and lacked guile and sharpness, although no one's fool. Waddell was boastful and lacked the same standard of intelligence or cunning as 'Tank'. The 'odd couple', indeed. In addition, Waddell was a drunk and loose-tongued and somewhat haggard. Hardly the dynamic duo.

Ludo Kennedy was interested in doing the Waddell experiment before the BBC cameras, but knew that far from going to England or abroad, Waddell would be lucky to get enough cash for a weekend in Rothesay, and a cheap one at that. Another meeting was arranged in Gibson's office and was attended by Kennedy, Scott, Vass, Murray, Gibson, Waddell, a friend of his called Farrell, and myself.

There was some significance to be attached to Farrell's presence in that he had been 'Tank's' co-accused in the case of the Richards murder in the previous year. Was he looking after 'Tank's' interests? And John Farrell had been the other person in my car at the Anvil Public House in Smithycroft Road, Glasgow!

Before the meeting I had lunched with Ludo and suggested that he should get Waddell going in talking about the non-disclosure of his accomplice. 'That presupposes that Waddell was there,' I stressed. 'This would be fresh evidence that Meehan had not been with him in Ayr. In that way, progress will be made, irrespective of the doomed truth drug experiment.'

Ludo listened carefully and agreed to the proposed course of action. He would start proceedings with the anonymity of Waddell's confederate.

Matters did not go according to plan. Ludo could not get to grips with Waddell. Farrell dominated the meeting and on occasions when I thought progress was being made, he (Farrell) would interject on Waddell's behalf. 'Don't answer that, Ian,' he would say. 'Tie them down to the cash!'

I felt that this 'pest' was in process of slamming yet another door in our faces. The meeting broke up in disarray.

David Scott assuaged my feelings later when he told me that he had Waddell on tape, anyway, and that he had mentioned matters that could only be known to a raider. Points like a luminous clock in the hallway and the photographs of a young child in the bottom drawer which he had ransacked. And it was all on tape.

Scott and Vass were quick to interview Ross, who confirmed the new points as being accurate. I was buoyant again.

Yet another coincidence reared its head. At around about this time I was instructed by a client who claimed he had been assaulted outside a public house in Glasgow's East End. He was after compensation from the Criminal Injuries Compensation Board—and his name was Donald Carmichael, no less. This was the first time that I had seen my old client since the Meehan trial. On that occasion Fairbairn had torn strips off him.

Neither Carmichael nor I mentioned Meehan's name in our several meetings covering his claim, although I must confess I was sorely tempted. I do remember looking at him and thinking, 'This man must know the truth, he must know that Meehan is innocent.'

We discussed his claim as though Ayr had never happened—in the friendliest of manners. His claim was satisfactorily negotiated over a period of four months and I resisted the temptation, at settlement, to ask him for the low-down on Ayr. Later, I blamed myself for not taking the bull by the horns—we would have been no worse off.

It is common knowledge that Waddell proceeded to confess to the Press—there were several 'exclusives'—no doubt for varying amounts of cash. Openly, on STV and BBC programmes, he confessed without the truth drug. Indeed, one could be excused for quoting, 'Methinks he doth confess too much.' He was glorying in the publicity. And his pseudo attempts at clearing Meehan at the expense of himself made him out to be a far nicer person than he ever was. Embarrassed as they must have been, the authorities treated his disclosures with derision, and would not be moved.

Funny, a year earlier, this was my golden dream. Just imagine a confession from Waddell and his public clearance of Meehan? Now it was becoming so common that it was a standing Press joke—'Which paper has his exclusive today?'

Like myself, Meehan must have been totally frustrated. Waddell realised that he could say what he liked and as much as he liked. He could, and he did, shout Meehan's innocence from the rooftops—the powers-that-be were not for listening, far less acting.

Admittedly, from time to time Waddell would retract his expressions of guilt, but this merely brought down more derision on his head. He was enjoying the publicity and no doubt the money as well. His face on TV and his Press photographs meant that he was no longer an insignificant East End punk, but a celebrity of sorts. He was pointed out in Glasgow streets and responded by trying to walk like Capone. But this fascinating Waddell chapter was now dead—it had done little to promote Meehan's cause.

It was readily said by police officers to me, and to others, 'Who in their right and sober senses would publicly and openly confess to murder through the media? If the authorities thought that there was anything in it, surely he would have been arrested by now.' It was hard to answer this, but, clearly, Waddell—cagey at first—became more and more confident as he seemed to realise that he had some sort of magic formula to bring about immunity from prosecution. He was later to learn a bitter lesson.

From our efforts on Meehan's behalf with the authorities, *vis à vis* Waddell (now an embarrassment all round), their attitude was that his plurality of confessions, then retractions, were inconclusive and that, in any event, there was at that moment in time no corroboration of them.

Mind you, I thought that the 'special knowledge' spoken of by Waddell—for example, the child's photograph in the drawer, which was confirmed by Ross—could afford the necessary corroboration.

I was not so much interested in having Waddell arraigned for trial as showing that the new developments must surely cast doubt on the validity of Meehan's conviction. I wasn't interested in retribution, but it seemed to me that the Crown would only budge from their intractable and intransigent position were they given the chance of putting someone inside in Meehan's place.

At a time when Waddell's media presence was on the decline, I remember seeing him in George Square as I was crossing diagonally from the court to the office. He was with his girlfriend and a young child. Scruffily dressed as always, he caught my eye, looked at me forlornly, outstretched both arms and shrugged as if to say, 'Well, I've tried, haven't I?'

But Waddell was later to be indicted for the Ayr murder, along with his friend, Dick, who was charged with conspiracy.

The Waddell chapter which started with such promise and excitement at Glasgow's Sheriff Court on the day he was sentenced to 12 months, ended up in a somewhat discredited way. Waddell was allowed to disappear into the obscurity he so richly deserved. At least for a year anyway. The irony was that there had been too many confessions, made too publicly. The normal circumstances—although Meehan's case was never average or normal—were that two confessions are better for the Crown than one, three better than two and so on. In Waddell's case this did not obtain. But the difference in evidential value is manifest. Pushing this simple legal proposition to its logical conclusion—what is the value of 15 confessions to, say, four million people, at least? So far as Meehan was concerned, totally worthless.

Very often Meehan was a topic of conversation with police officers and myself. Officer after officer pooh-poohed my pleas. Later on, when the street dogs were again barking out Meehan's innocence, the same officers would say, 'Well, perhaps Meehan was not one of the two in the house, but he was still involved. He was outside in a car just in case the safe had to be blown.'

These officers can be excused for making this observation—Lord Hunter was tempted to make a similar point in 1982 in his report. My reply was to the effect, 'That was *not* the evidence on which he was convicted.' In any event, a McGuinness did not require a Meehan to crack a safe—he could have taught Meehan a few 'wrinkles' on the subject.

There were other police officers who encouraged my public stand and would say to me, 'Don't give up, you're right.'

The whole Waddell saga and failure was thoroughly canvassed at our second 'Free Paddy Meehan Committee' meeting. The meeting was lengthy, progress slow and there was little to report to assembled Pressmen in our terse communique.

During this time I had been invited to speak at numerous church organisations, literary societies, Rotaries, Round Tables, Inner Wheels etc. about the law and individual cases. Meehan's case always took pride of place and most audiences responded. Most listeners showed a healthy interest in the case and I was plied with a miscellany of pertinent questions.

Yes, slowly, but steadily, efforts were being made by me to ensure that Meehan, although languishing in Peterhead, (for the most part in solitary confinement) would not be forgotten and allowed to fade into obscurity. The year 1973 had started with a fire—and finished with a dying ember. I was, however, becoming less of a figure of fun, so far as the Glasgow Police Force were concerned.

In early 1974 I met Frank McElhone, the Gorbals MP, again, this time with my friend Len Murray. We dined at the Bruce Hotel, East Kilbride, and returned to my Bothwell home. The purpose was to assist Frank to prepare an adjournment debate before the House of Commons about the Meehan fiasco, in the hope that this would compel the Scottish Secretary to prepare answers for the benefit of the House.

I knew that we had a number of Members on our side, including my good friend Winnie Ewing. She had interested herself in this case from very early on—she knew that there was something wrong with the conviction. Frank, Len and I spent a number of hours preparing the way for the debate and marshalling all the salient and cogent facts.

On 20 March 1974 Frank rose in the House of Commons and delivered his address with his usual aplomb and dedication. Regrettably, the time was 5.05 a.m. and at that uninspiring hour the House was virtually empty. Frank said:

There can be few, if any, other cases in the legal history of Scotland or England of a man serving a sentence of life imprisonment for a crime to which another man had confessed in incontrovertible detail. Even if there had been no such confession, the events which emerged and the evidence which has become available since the conviction casts the greatest doubts upon the validity of the original verdict. Who in this House would ever say that upon the evidence now available a jury would ever convict Patrick Meehan? The situation has disturbed the conscience of many within the legal profession, persons of standing and responsibility.

He went on to describe the paucity and frailty of the Crown evidence, the prejudice surrounding the trial, and the withdrawal of the special defence of impeachment of Waddell.

McElhone gave details of two of the Waddell confessions and pointed out that he betrayed knowledge of the description, design and content of the bungalow, as to be known only to one of the raiders.

He next referred to a part of the Crown Office statement—and it is worth repeating: 'With the death of Griffiths and the apprehension of Patrick Meehan, the police are no longer looking for any other persons suspected of implication in the incident concerning Mr and Mrs Ross at Ayr.'

Frank asked: 'With such prejudice, what need is there for evidence?' He finished by thanking Fairbairn, Murray and myself—'a solicitor at the trial who has been convinced of Meehan's innocence ever since he was convicted five years ago'.

He was followed by the then Minister of State, Bruce Millan, replying on behalf of the Scottish Secretary, Willie Ross. Millan said he recognised McElhone's concern, and that of others, about this case. He promised that the whole matter would be further investigated.

14

Throughout the rest of that year and the next, and those before, for that matter, I was frequently visited in the office by Betty Meehan and her son, Pat. They were tireless and endless workers on my client's behalf. At times it was embarrassing—so often I had so little to say about the matter of developments. On occasions, I publicly confess, I had to advise my receptionist that I was 'out'—when I was hiding in my room. I did not find out until much later that the son, Pat, who worked in the bank opposite my office, overlooking me, would check to see if I was at my desk, before crossing the road!

You can imagine the melancholy feelings permeating the whole office when one or other of them appeared. My staff knew that they would leave the office with little more confidence than when they arrived.

A succession of blank, powerful walls constantly faced us. I could not even tell them of the sporadic meetings I was now having with 'Tank' McGuinness—for the reasons I have stated.

During these difficult times I was dealing with a client who had become ungrateful (he had no idea the time being spent on his behalf), sullen and truculent. He expected that all other matters be dropped, save his case. He was also unrealistic in the extreme. He formed the view in his tortured mind that Fairbairn and I had acted against his interests at the trial, having been 'got at' by the Special Branch. In short, that we had betrayed our client for the benefit of other mysterious authorities. It would be difficult to level a greater charge against members of the legal profession. Yes, there was every excuse—and that was the main one—to do a 'Pontius Pilate' and wash my hands of the whole sorry affair.

Before finally leaving the Waddell confessions, and progressing to those of McGuinness, let me lay out the extent and enormity of them and the significance in my eyes.

Waddell drew a sketched plan of the interior of 2 Blackburn Place, Ayr, which was later confirmed as accurate by Abraham Ross. After the BBC and STV confessions, Waddell went on to confess to Gordon Ayres and Charles Beaton of the *Scottish Daily Record*, and George Forbes and Jack Wallace of the *Scottish Daily News*. In all, these confessions were telescoped into a three-year period from 1973 to 1975.

There were many significant factors in these confessions of Waddell—certainly crucial to me—in which certain of the information supplied must have been known only to the bungalow raiders. Many of the factors had not been touched upon at the Meehan trial, and it is unlikely, to say the least, that Meehan would have waited so long before feeding such 'secret' information to someone else.

The following is a consensus of the salient points made by Waddell in the course of his numerous confessions to various people:

That Meehan and Griffiths were entirely innocent

That it was a two-man job only

That William McIntyre should have gone with him, but that he had taken cold feet when he learned that violence might be involved (a tie-up job)—and, as a result, a well-known 'professional' was conscripted late on in the proceedings

That Andrew Dick, who had first told him about the prospect, had sat up all night with William McIntyre at Dick's Law Street flat to 'provide each other with an alibi'

That he and his recently recruited accomplice had left Glasgow in a silver Cortina car, hired by his colleague

That both of them had had a meal in an Ayr cafe, having arrived there with plenty of time to spare

That the robbery was 'never supposed to end in murder'

That they broke into the house at about 1 a.m. and left (with his accomplice driving) after about 5.30 a.m., when it was daylight and there was less opportunity of being pulled up by the police

That a gold watch had been snatched from the wrist of Mrs Ross

That his accomplice had taken Ross's car keys, had gone into his garage to take his car (red in colour), but that he could not get it started

That the colour of the Ross quilts was pink

That his accomplice had cut the telephone wires by standing up on the shed and using ladders; that they entered the house through the front window, using a jemmy to prise it open

That there was a large, shiny, wooden floor in the hallway, and also a clock with luminous hands and figures, and a table with flowers on it

That the Rosses were in separate beds, with the man nearest the window

That he went for the woman, and his accomplice went for the man; that Mr Ross struggled and got out of bed and his accomplice shouted, 'Get this cunt off me,' calling him either Pat or Jim

That these common Christian names were deliberately adopted beforehand—as is the usual practice in such 'jobs' when there must, of necessity, be conversation, for example, in endeavours to obtain the safe key, etc

That he did not know Griffiths or Meehan at that time

That Mr Ross continued fighting, 'So I hit him with the jemmy'

That Mrs Ross just lay there in bed, although she shouted, asking if her husband was all right

That they tied them up using a clothes rope which had been hanging up in the garden; that his accomplice left the room and came back with a small case full of money

That he found £1,800 (consisting of new ten pound notes) in the hip pocket of the man's trousers which were hanging over a chair in the bedroom

That, earlier, they had asked where the safe was and he said that he did not have one; that they were wearing balaclava hoods and they put on the light

That they flung a pink quilt over the man's head and a pillowslip over hers

That there was a safe under the stairs

That his accomplice opened the safe with a long mortice-type key; that they were in the house for quite a few hours, leaving at 5.30 a.m.

That when he (Waddell) was ransacking one of the drawers he had seen a photograph of an elderly man with two young children

That there was a 'wee' alarm clock sitting on the kitchen window

That there was a key in the back door

That they had a drink from an open bottle of whisky in the kitchen

That their 'haul' was much in excess of the figure disclosed in Meehan's indictment—that is, £1,800

That the woman next door had spotted him outside the Ross bungalow at about 11 p.m. on the Saturday evening

That he had thrown ammonia in the face of Mrs Ross (thus the significance of the additional medical statements at his own trial by Professor Gilbert Forbes and others)

That he had seen a light-tan suit in the bedroom wardrobe

That his accomplice had left the house after trying, unsuccessfully, to start Ross's car—and had come back with the hired one (which had been parked some distance away near to a hotel)

That this hotel was the Savoy Park on Racecourse Road, about one half-mile away from the Ross bungalow

That his accomplice had picked him up and that he had told him that he (the accomplice) had been 'pulled' by the 'busies', but had handled matters all right

That he had told Mrs Ross, before leaving, that he would telephone for an ambulance, as she kept asking if her husband was all right

That they returned to Glasgow the long way, namely by the A74 and 'split the loot' on a lay-by on the Edinburgh Road

That he had got a taxi and returned to the house of his friend (Donald Carmichael's), who had already promised to supply him with an alibi

That he later visited a bar manager who let him off-load the 'hot' money and later provided him with a lawyer (Mr Carlin) after the matter had escalated into a murder enquiry

That he had agreed in 1972 to be examined under the 'truth drug', provided he was not asked to identify his accomplice

That he spoke to Beltrami about the 'truth drug' idea and that 'maybe I felt sorry for Meehan—I would like to see Meehan released as long as I don't go in'

That he was surprised when he later learned that the woman had died, and thought that it would have been the man

And so the statement went on . . . I have only summarised it. It was all amazingly accurate, hanging together well. And it was information given—long before he was put on trial—which was checked with Abraham Ross sometime before his death.

The next-door neighbour who had seen someone at 11 p.m. also confirmed this matter. Yes, confirmation of the many unsolicited points came from Ross, but still nothing was done by the authorities, apart from stating that there was insufficient evidence to go against Waddell, far less free Meehan.

One can understand why the confessions gradually became bolder and more detailed, on the realisation then that the criminal authorities showed so little interest in them—and, indeed, seemed to give them the 'Nelson Eye'.

Incidentally, some months after his murder acquittal, and weeks after his release from prison for the assault conviction, as a result of which he was serving an 18-month sentence at the time of his murder arraignment, Waddell had the audacity and temerity to confess his guilt yet once more in the Glasgow *Evening Times*, and that without payment of any sort. This was in the month of April, 1977, and he said:

I want to tell the whole truth. If I tell the whole story it would show that I did it. I am prepared to take a lie detector test, or have the truth drug administered to me, along with Meehan. I want to get round the table with everyone involved in the case to get the truth told. I want to start a new life with all this behind me. I did it, but I have no conscience about the murder. I left them both bound but alive, and I do not think that that is murder.

15

I was still receiving nasty letters from Meehan who was still in Peterhead. I wondered why I should continue to act while receiving such unfair abuse. Probably, on his behalf, I cherished 'the importance of being innocent'.

Enough, however, about Waddell—Waddell, the weaker in the partnership. Let's now turn to his much more professional running-mate, 'Tank' McGuinness.

The Anvil conversation, when 'Tank' mentioned Meehan's name to me for the very first time, took place in late November of 1972. As I saw him enter the Anvil pub with Farrell I wondered when I would see McGuinness again. He would not surely leave me hanging in air after broaching the delicate subject with me. I did not have too long to wait.

Towards the end of January 1973, several months after our minimal, but revealing, conversation in Smithycroft Road, 'Tank' called at my office without appointment. When I was given his name by my receptionist, I perked up, realising that I had no current matters for him (like outstanding cases). I hoped that his call might concern Meehan—and I did not have to wait long for confirmation.

He sat down on the chair on the other side of my large desk, the same seat he would occupy so often in the future.

'Yes?' I said expectantly, trying to appear and look my normal self.

I hardly looked up when he said, as his opening gambit, 'Do you still have a copy of Meehan's indictment?'

Within seconds I was able to produce it—his papers were always to hand. I offered it to him. He took it and read it very carefully. I waited and wondered what on earth the point of this exercise might be. After all, no one knew the indictment better than I.

He seemed to be concentrating on the list of productions, of which there were many. Minutes later he returned it to me and stared at me with those penetrating eyes. 'I see that Meehan was never charged with stealing Ross's car keys—no mention of them.'

I felt let down and disappointed and thought, 'Is this the best he can come up with?' I could not see that there was any point to make. I asked him for the significance of his point. He replied by putting a question to me. 'Have these keys ever been mentioned before now?'

'No, never.'

He became suddenly animated, saying, 'Because his car keys were taken. The police must know that, as must Abraham Ross, and yet there is no mention in this document.'

Thinking that the conversation was becoming a little anticlimactic, if not a trifle mundane, I decided to take a risk—after all, Meehan had nothing more to lose, in any event. 'How can you be so certain about Ross's car keys?' I blurted out.

'Tank' replied at once, 'Because I took them.'

This was his first direct statement of involvement. I thought quickly about how to follow it up. I realised that the present situation was unique and did not want him to clam up now. I tried to be as casual as possible—as if this were an everyday occurrence—and took no notes. I never did take written notes, for fear it might scare him off. Many moons later I did sketch a plan, when he tried to show me where he had hidden both of Rachel Ross's rings and the car keys.

I asked him why he had taken the car keys, as I told him, there had been a getaway car used. 'What would be the need?'

He answered no more questions that day, blandly ignoring mine. 'Surely,' he said, 'you could make use of the fact that Ross's car keys were stolen, and that that fact has never yet been mentioned by the authorities.'

I said I would think about it but I would be grateful for more detailed information about the murder.

Again he ignored my last plea, saying simply, 'It was never murder. My accomplice agreed to telephone 999 after we were well away from the scene. He bungled it.'

He seemed restless and disinterested now and I formed the view, correctly, that he was telling me that this consultation was now over. I decided on a parting shot, 'Was Ian Waddell your accomplice?'

He did not reply but looked at me in a meaningful way—the suggestion being that I was becoming too inquisitive. I could almost hear him thinking, 'Watch it.'

I recoiled. He got up and walked out. The meeting was over.

How well I remember my excitement at the time. The daunting fact was that Waddell's confessions were far too public. 'Tank's' confession to me was private, confidential and for my ears only. This added to the frustration. Could it now be that real things were actually happening?

I could not tell a soul, such is the bond of confidentiality between solicitor and client. I now had a secret that was to weigh heavily on my shoulders for more than three years.

The rule of complete confidentiality between solicitor and client has, however, its exception. Let us assume that a client gives his solicitor erroneous, lying and misleading information to put before a court—say, in a plea of mitigation of sentence. For example, he might instruct his lawyer to state that he is in employment or, perhaps, he is self-employed, with a number of employees dependent on him . . . as a result of which he might avoid disqualification from driving or a period of imprisonment. In the event of a criminal prosecution of the client on a charge of perverting the course of justice, it would not be in order for his solicitor to plead confidentiality and so refuse to speak or give a statement to the authorities embracing the incorrect information and the source of it.

As a matter of commonsense, if this were not the case then no such person could be brought to justice for misleading the court in this manner. To sum up this exception to the confidentiality rule, it has to be said that where a client manipulates a solicitor—indeed, compromises him—to assist in the commission of a crime (albeit unknowingly on the part of the agent) then the client cannot claim confidentiality in the interests of justice.

I decided to do nothing in the meantime about the car keys.

If I had gone to the police—as Lord Hunter in his report was later to indicate that I should have done—what would have happened? McGuinness would have denied any conversation about Meehan and the powers-that-be would almost certainly have thought that this was another manoeuvre (because that's what they thought about the truth drug) by me, a very biased protagonist of Meehan's.
I could only wait and hope that 'Tank' would return. Somehow I felt that he would, and I checked that his name had been included in my receptionist's day book. It had.

Months later, he returned. He asked me if I had done anything about the car keys. I said, 'No.' I told him that I needed more information of such a type and nature that it could only come from one of those involved—information that was never public knowledge. Even with this, the authorities would probably have claimed that I gleaned it from Meehan. I asked 'Tank' why he had taken the car keys in the first place, because that chapter was still a mystery to me. After all, why should he?

He was more responsive on this occasion, although he did not answer at once. The matter was rapidly becoming a 'cat and mouse' affair. 'Meehan is entirely innocent, not that I ever liked him. If they can convict an innocent man of murder and then do nothing about it, they could do the same to me or anyone. Meehan's case must be sorted out before it's too late. They cannot be allowed to get away with it!'

I gathered by 'they' he meant the authorities.

He then referred somewhat disparagingly to some of the evidence and said, 'I've never known of anyone set up for murder, at least anyone entirely innocent, like Meehan.'

Not all of our 'clandestine' meetings took place within the safety and security of my office. On occasions he would seek me out at the local Sheriff Court where he knew I spent a great deal of time. On those occasions—he was always alone—I would usher him to a place out of public earshot. I did not relish this 'cloak and dagger' approach and often wondered if this strange part of my life would go with me, a secret, to the grave.

I allowed him to talk and decided not to put pointed questions to him like, 'Was Ian Waddell with you?'

The thought occurred to me on this, the second, office meeting, anent Meehan, that I would have to tape him—but what good was it? How could I use it anyway? I quickly dispelled the thought. I knew that I daren't. This would be considered trickery and most certainly 'not cricket'. I must admit that the same thought did recur over the next few years. I even saw an appropriate place to put a tape-recorder under my large desk. These were, however, only thoughts, and nothing was ever done about them.

I knew my office was five storeys up and that there would be little interference, and that the device could be secreted, easily, close to the seat he always used. However, such information as I was being given was in strict confidence, and taping 'Tank' would have been of little credit to my profession. Repeatedly, I arrived at this conclusion—but, as useless as the tape would have been, it would have been reassuring to possess it.

Perhaps the reader can imagine my extreme frustration—a murderer spitting out his most private and deepest thoughts to me, a solicitor not openly and publicly allowed to clear a victim of his callously criminal acts. During his lifetime my lips must remain sealed—and he was certainly a fit and healthy client who might well outlive me.

I was brought back to earth with a bang. . . .

'Our getaway car was parked in a side-street about half a mile away, towards Ayr. My accomplice (no name of Waddell yet) was supposed to drive it to the side of Ross's house in Racecourse Road after we had opened the safe, but he was covered in Mrs Ross's blood.

'The job lasted much longer than we planned. Ross was stubborn. So I decided to go for the car because of the state of the other man.

'I was afraid of being stopped on the road at that time in the morning so I took Ross's car keys and tried to start his car. I intended to drive it to the getaway car and leave it there. Ross's car wouldn't start. I tried it a few times.

'I did not go back into the house but put his keys in my pocket, crossed some gardens and jumped down into Racecourse Road.'

At this meeting he made no mention of the police and their patrol car.

He then went on to reiterate what he had said at our first meeting, about the strange omission of the car keys from the charge and the evidence.

I realised that little real progress was being made towards Meehan's release. I thought the meeting was almost over—they seldom took long—and tried to prolong it by saying, 'You could always go to the authorities yourself?'

'Never,' he rasped. 'Listen, if I were inside for a safe-blowing committed by Meehan, he would never come forward to help me. He would say it was my hard luck. After all, I didn't put him inside.'

I then suggested—more in hope than anything else—that, with his permission, I could go to the authorities and tell them what I knew, without disclosing his identity, and suggest that, in return for a full detailed confession, they might consider the question of immunity from prosecution in the interest of justice to Meehan.

'They would never agree to that—it would cause too much embarrassment to the police.'

On this somewhat negative note our second meeting ended and he scurried out of the room.

If he had agreed to the latter course, I might have been in difficulties in that the powers-that-be might have demanded the identity of my informant. I could not, and would not, have told them, and wondered what their attitude might then have been towards me.

As in the first instance, there was no arrangement made for another meeting.

Shortly after this, 'Tank' was charged along with John 'Gypsy' Winning, a staunch pal, with drug offences. Bail was granted, but before long I was to receive word that proceedings were to be abandoned. 'Tank's' luck was certainly holding. A third man had been charged and the Crown proceeded against him—he was a relation of 'Tank's'. This third man had the privilege of having both Winning and McGuinness as defence witnesses—and with their considerable experience, my task was, indeed, easy.

We were now into 1974 and our meetings continued to take place both in the office and, as I have said, the Sheriff Court. McGuinness was always on about progress in the Meehan affair. He was anxious that progress should be made and that I should achieve this. Alas, there was not a great deal of progress, although Waddell had already had a lot to say publicly about his part in the matter. It was almost as if he (Waddell) were defying the authorities to do something, in the definite knowledge that they would not.

I told 'Tank' about our committee, chaired by Ludovic Kennedy, a well-known writer and TV personality. Meehan was still capturing the headlines.

Between our second meeting and the very last, in late 1975—a memorable one when he disappeared out of my life in such a manner as to cause me a great deal of personal concern for my own safety— the whole Ayr plot unfolded, link by link. What I am about to relate is the gist of our many meetings.

'Tank' had been terribly concerned about Meehan's plight and the fact that nothing appeared to be done about it. He continued to place an undue significance on his theft of the car keys—but he went on. . . .

He had been brought into the scheme late, because someone had pulled out; he was never 100 per cent in favour of his accomplice— later he did identify him to me as being Waddell—as he did not think he had the necessary experience and nerve for a 'tie-up' job, which was somewhat specialised. He also talked too much and drank too much. 'Tank' had never worked with Waddell in the past and would certainly never do so in the future. 'Look at the way that drunken idiot is blabbing to the Press—he'll get us both done,' he told me.

He had fallen out with Waddell. They no longer spoke, nor

would they. There had only been two of them in Ayr—'Tank' had never heard of Griffiths, far less worked with him. He would never have worked with Meehan in any event because he had no time for him and thought that he (Meehan) would give information to suit his own ends. In other words, he did not trust Meehan one inch.

'Tank' had hired the getaway car in his own name from a garage in Edinburgh, using his own driving licence. The beauty of this was that, if stopped, he could satisfy anyone as to the authenticity of his possession of it.

After they split up, the plan was that Waddell should phone 999, and anonymously advise the authorities of the job in view of the ages of the victims. Waddell couldn't even do this right—he bungled it in his panic and 'Tank' had not found out about that until it was too late. Causing death had been furthest from his mind, but, once again, Waddell had over-reacted with Mrs Ross. McGuinness told me, 'I should have phoned the ambulance myself.'

This was almost a plea to me. He later told me that he had been picked up by the 'busies' in Racecourse Road and he was lucky that they hadn't seen him jump from the garden or it would have been all over. He was then taken to the Ayr bus depot. He had given a 'snide' name and this was accepted by the two policemen.

He had returned the hired car to Edinburgh and hired another one from the same firm. He had driven to England because the 'heat' was on.

On his return, sometime later, he had heard of Meehan's arrest. 'I had just driven past Gretna when I heard it on the car radio, for the first time, that Meehan had appeared in court that day charged with the Ayr murder.' He went on to say that he could hardly accept the news—it was incredible. He felt that a serious mistake had obviously been made and that, in time, Meehan would be released. In short, he felt that Meehan would get a 'lie-in', as he had done in the Richards case years later, of about two months, before being released on the grounds of insufficient evidence.

Several times 'Tank' chastised himself in my presence for 'doing a stupid thing'. He went on to tell me that he had lodged a substantial sum of money in his own bank account in Shettleston Road shortly after returning from England. 'I probably did that, stupid as it was, because Meehan had been arrested, Griffiths was dead, and the police were not looking for anyone else. I was in the clear.' 'Tank' had been unemployed for many years and realised that he had been extremely foolish.

It is interesting to note that when I checked this out after his death, his address in the bank book was that of his former residence—Waddell Court in Glasgow's South Side. How's that for yet another coincidence!

16

Despite getting information from 'Tank', I remained powerless. As I have said, 'Tank' was a man who knew little of fear, yet, in 1975, when our meetings were drawing to an end, it was clear that pressure was being brought to bear on him.

I felt that 'underworld' friends of Meehan may have found out about our meetings—indeed, they may have been responsible for 'Tank' coming to me in the first place—and decided that 'Tank' had not gone far enough to assist Meehan.

Although Meehan decried violence in any form, he was well known to the Glasgow underworld and persons to whom violence was second nature. It may be that one or more of them—I think only one would be enough—had possibly prompted 'Tank' to see me at first.

Matters crystalised in early 1975 when two masked men arrived at his door late at night. Fortunately for him, he was not there, but his wife, Agnes, and his daughter, Elizabeth, underwent a dreadful experience in his absence. One of the men was armed with a sawn-off shotgun. The house was searched for McGuinness. The shotgun was fired into a cupboard, badly damaging it—probably to prove that it was loaded. Yes, they meant business. Then they left.

'Tank' told me about the incident shortly afterwards—he even gave me the names of the two hooded men, who were underworld 'heavies'—and was able to tell me that they were paid handsomely (he told me the figure) to cause him injury. Not surprisingly, he had not given the names to the police who had interviewed him about the fearsome incident.

He felt that the plan had been to surprise him, then shoot him about the knees, crippling him and thereby inducing him to clear Meehan, or else.

The irony is that Meehan would not have approved of this, in any event.

'Tank' was not so much afraid for himself as he was infuriated that his family had been brought into the matter. His first reaction had been to arm himself—that would have caused little difficulty—and go after both men, but I urged him against this revenge-filled task. But I will tell you what he did later on.

The effect, I think, of this incident was that he gave me a fresh lead in the Meehan case—one that could bear fruit at last.

When stopped by the police Panda patrol he had in his pockets the Ross car keys and Rachel's two rings. He had successfully bluffed the matter out, like the pro he was, telling them that he had been at the Orange Walk march in Irvine on the Saturday, having earlier visited his daughter there who was on holiday (That was true and was later confirmed).

He had given, as I said earlier, a 'snide' name, not too unlike McGuinness—I think, 'McGuigan'. He was given a lift to the Ayr bus depot by the police to catch the first Glasgow bus. He was not searched—he could hardly believe his luck. They accepted what he said without checking. The officers had not recognised him, despite his earlier Ayrshire crimes.

After leaving him there the police drove off. He had, of course, to double back to the getaway car. He went into Wellington Square (the site of the Sheriff Court) and used a deserted dirt track at the side of the nearby shore links. This track has a wall to its left (heading south) and the start of the links to its right.

One must remember that 'Tank' was neither a coherent nor an articulate speaker, and would often go off at a tangent. Sometimes there was no logical link between one sentence and another.

He said that while running along this track he noticed the lights of a hotel (The Savoy Park) situated in Racecourse Road. He ran up the steps at the first break of wall to his left, and panicked when he realised he still had the stolen items in his pocket. Now he was re-entering civilisation from the deserted links . . . what if he were again seen by the two 'busies' in the Panda?

He was still a distance north of the getaway car and would have to re-enter Racecourse Road. He stopped before re-entering and, in the darkness, only illuminated by the distant hotel lights, he picked up a heavy manhole cover and secreted the two rings in a narrow culvert-type ridge or sill immediately under the outer rim of the drain. The ridge was covered in muck, which would assist in ensuring that the rings did not fall down into the drain-water several feet below.

Again, I was given only the barest of details by 'Tank'—I gained fuller knowledge later by visiting the drains, as I will reveal.

McGuinness had replaced the top of the drain and run off. He then remembered the car keys, picked up another drain cover and dealt with the keys in the very same way.

Now stripped of the incriminating evidence, he felt much more secure. He did not see the police again, returned to the getaway car, drove it to the Ross house, picked up Waddell and the stolen cash, and left Ayr. His luck had held.

When he told me about the keys and the two rings I became quite excited.

If these items were found six years after the murder the police could hardly make out that I had been given the information by Meehan—why should he wait so long before telling me?

'Tank' drew a rough sketch plan in my office, starting with the bus depot and working back from there. I did not ask any questions but just looked at the sketch drawn in his own fair hand. Evidence at last?

I asked him to recover the items and he said he would go down with a friend to look at the area—he had not been there since that night—and he would then come back to see me in two days' time. This he did—but he had not found them. 'I'm not sure where the drains were, it was very, very dark and so long ago,' he said.

I told him that I would visit Ayr and recover the rings. I would need help, I told him, and asked if I could introduce him to my Office Manager, Michael MacDonald. I told him that Michael knew all about Meehan's case. To my surprise, he agreed and, hurriedly, after the briefest of messages, I brought Michael into my room, where he met 'Tank' for the first time. This, too, was a breakthrough—someone else in on the plot.

We questioned McGuinness, added to the sketch plan, and tried to tie him down more as to the location of the drains. As said earlier, he was far from a fluent speaker and was of little help. It was a bit like looking for a needle in a haystack, but it had to be done—and was.

But I was still dubious about his statement of being stopped by the police in Racecourse Road and wondered if he were having me on.

After all, had I not phoned Gall at Ayr Police Headquarters about this possibility prior to the trial without success?

I remember saying to McGuinness earlier, 'Are you sure you were stopped by the police because I have checked this out with them?'

He said, 'Of course, I'm sure.'

I remember, too, being sceptical about the possibility of finding the rings and keys which had been deposited on narrow mud-caked shelves six inches below street level—after six years. I said, 'These drains will be cleaned out from time to time.'

'Yes, but the suction machine would not affect items on the shelves.' McGuinness said.

'Tank' was very confident that all three items could be recovered—but not by him.

In addition to his speech and thought deficiencies, 'Tank' was inclined to mumble and 'eat' some of his words. Another difficulty was my maintaining a casual approach, which meant that neither did I write anything down, nor did I look at him much at our meetings.

I wondered what I would do if we found any or all of the stolen items. I confess I felt it would be a lot easier if we did not trace them. We could not hold on to those stolen goods—that would be reset—but would be required to take them to Ayr Police Headquarters.

I would be asked on whose information I had commenced the search. I could not tell them. Being stolen goods, they would insist that I should and threaten me with a charge of 'attempting to pervert the course of justice'. There would be much hostility, as there always had been at Ayr Police Headquarters.

I could tell them that the information had come from a client who had confessed to me that he had done the Ayr job along with Ian Waddell. I would tell them the reason for his depositing the two items in two drains—because of the police intervention in Racecourse Road, which I still thought to be the weakness of the story.

The uncertainty of what would happen in the police station worried me—a good reason for bringing Ludovic Kennedy into the frame.

I would tell them that Meehan was not my informant—he would hardly have waited six years to bring about such a ruse.

The more I thought about it the more I hoped that we would find nothing but an attempt clearly required to be made by us. Supposing we had been seen by police officers acting suspiciously and examining drains? I would be asked why I had not given the police the information and allowed them to search.

There are two reasons why I did not, in fact do any of this—(1) had nothing been found I would have looked foolish, and (2) I did not know what they would do with them if they found them—after all 'Tank's' allegation was that two policemen stopped him and there was no official record of this anywhere. Would these recovered items be allowed to 'disappear' and so vital evidence be lost?

I knew full well that the police seemed happy about the conclusion of the case on Meehan's conviction. Would they want to re-open it?

I did not realise there were so many drains in the area . . . .

Ludovic and I, while Michael MacDonald kept a look-out, took up about ten drain covers—there were many more between the Savoy Park Hotel in Racecourse Road and Blackburn Place. Some of the tops had not been removed, it seemed, for many a year. And they were very, very heavy.

It must have looked strange—Ludo and I, both quite well-known, on our hands and knees, searching drains. It was a filthy task and in no time our hands were covered in muck.

Sure enough, there was a concave-shaped narrow sill or ledge about three-quarters of an inch in width right round the rectangular top of the drain, immediately under the place where the cover had been.

We searched a few in Racecourse Road (both sides) near the Savoy Park Hotel, as well as some in Fairfield Road and Wheatfield Road.

I was convinced that the getaway car (the Cortina) was parked in Wheatfield Road. We were keen, we were anxious—and we were unsuccessful. We spent about three hours there.

I did not tell Ludo who my informant was, merely that he was the second man (both of us knew that Waddell was the first). Ludo, however, fully appreciated the clear significance and value of the evidence, were it to be found by us.

It turned out that nothing was found. Our presence was not brought to the attention of the local police and the three of us left Ayr thinking that, once again, we had been thwarted. I was, and am, convinced that 'Tank' was telling the truth and thought that I might return later to check a few more drains. This never happened—there were other even more dramatic developments to follow . . . .

The items had been hidden in pitch darkness so long ago, and 'Tank' was by no means certain where they were. I remember seeing Ludo down groping for the cherished items. I remember thinking that if the police arrived I might be better off if I said that I had had information from an anonymous source by telephone. A white lie, perhaps, but less dangerous to me.

Next day, 'Tank' came to the office and heard about our lack of success. He agreed to go down himself that night and try to recover them. I was pleased and agreed to meet him in a few days' time. On this occasion we made an appointment which was kept, but he returned to say that he was unable to recover them. 'It was very dark and I was in a panic when I hid them. Why are there so many drains in that area?'

By this time Ludo had almost finished a book he was writing on the case and I asked McGuinness if it would be in order to incorporate in Ludovic's book that one of my clients had confessed to me and had cleared completely Meehan and Griffiths.

McGuinness thought for several minutes and then said 'No.' He added, 'If that information were published in a book Waddell will know that I, too, had opened my mouth. This could cause Waddell to panic.' And he walked out of my office.

I spoke to Michael MacDonald and told him that what 'Tank' had said at the previous meeting was highly confidential and could never be disclosed by him—to anyone.

The last time I saw 'Tank' was in September of 1975. He came in again without appointment and appeared agitated. He looked at me menacingly—I had never seen him quite like this before. 'The busies,' he said, 'have been following me since yesterday. They followed me to the bank today.'

I expressed little surprise at this outburst and said simply. 'You're a well-known criminal. You, of all people, must know that Criminal Intelligence keeps a close eye on persons such as you. You must be under surveillance from time to time.'

His whole manner and approach indicated that he thought that I had gone to the police and told them about the meetings.

'Why now, when the pressure is building up over Meehan?' he asked.

'I have told no one of your involvement,' I reassured him. 'You have been my client for a long time and I would never betray you.'

He interjected, 'It's too much of a coincidence.'

I decided not to protest too much and tried not to look in any way nervous or upset. I tried to hide my feelings. Still staring insanely, he got up and left without comment. I was never to see him again.

Knowing of his violent propensities, when I later left my office I felt more than a little dejected. I had a drink with my partners but, to be truthful, my mind was not on the conversation.

Later that night I found difficulty in sleeping and remember getting up at around 1 a.m., pulling back the curtains of my upstairs bedroom and opening one of the windows.

I was looking for the rone pipe and was pleased to note that this means of access to my bedroom was sufficiently far away as to render its use, by scaling, totally impractical. The rone pipe was at least eight feet away from the nearest oriel window.

My wife wondered what I was doing. I told her that I had heard a noise. I was a little less anxious by then.

17

It was no wonder 'Tank' did not come back . . . .

On 11 November 1975 he was interviewed by Chief Superintendent John MacDougall at Temple police office. He told the police that he knew Waddell only by sight and reputation. When questioned, he said he had never spoken to him.

> ' During the past three years I have seen reports in the Press that Waddell was responsible for the murder at Ayr. He had confessed to reporters. I have never given information to the police in my life and I never will assist them in criminal matters.
>
> I am not going to say anything about the Ayr murder—but all I will say is that Waddell should be arrested and you will find out that he will soon change his story. Most people know that he only makes these confessions for money. There was a lot of talk of Waddell during the Meehan trial. I know he was 'done' for perjury.
>
> The talk now is that he could not be done again because the police do not know which story is the true one.
>
> I'm very annoyed but not in the least worried about being questioned about the Ayr murder. I have been asked if I can remember where I was on the nights of 6/7 July '69. [*It should have been 5/6—the police got that wrong, too.*] I have no idea where I was on those dates and I had nothing to do with attacking the old Jewish couple. Any suggestion that I did is just ridiculous.'

He was promptly released by the police. Some time ago I mentioned how 'Tank' had seen me shortly after the underworld visit to his home and their attempt to cripple him. I had dissuaded him from seeking revenge. Instead, he went to a psychiatrist in an endeavour to calm himself down and so curb his normal instinct for retribution.

He attended the psychiatrist on several occasions—after his death I recovered his attendance card and handed this over to the police investigators. 'Tank' had visited the psychiatric units of both Duke Street and Woodilee Hospitals from October 1974. He failed to keep his last appointment in April 1975.

It was noted that he was depressed and talked of committing a murder and suicide. He mentioned fears for the safety of his wife and daughter (not himself). He had a great urge to kill the two men who had entered his home and terrified his family. He was diagnosed as a psychopathic personality, who could commit murder.

This information, of course, was obtained after his death in March 1976, through the good offices of two senior police officers, Bell and MacDougall, following information given to them by his family and myself.

We are nearing the end of the memorable 'Tank' chapter. . . .

In early March 1976 I read in the newspapers that 'Tank' had been found beaten and unconscious in Janefield Street, in Glasgow's Parkhead district. He was removed to the Royal Infirmary in a coma. He never recovered consciousness and died there 13 days later.

His was what one might describe as a freak death—no motive was ever established. I felt that the Asian doctor who first examined him in casualty, smelling drink from his breath and seeing the scars on his tough-looking face, diagnosed his case as that of a hard man who had over-imbibed. He was kept lying on his back, without further examination, for perhaps too long. The post mortem disclosed that he had been punched and had cracked his skull on the pavement of Janefield Street, close to Celtic Football Club's ground.

Much was to follow his death—the turning point of the Meehan case.

In McGuinness's favour, he had done all that he could for Meehan— although he disliked him immensely—short of putting his own neck in the proverbial noose, and few would have expected him to do that.

Looking back, my many brief meetings with him were exciting, and such a situation must surely be unique in the annals of criminal law. Although I had fears for myself after our last meeting, these proved to be groundless. I know that I will never again be in the position I found myself from 1973 to 1975, but, on reflection, this was perhaps the most exciting period of my law career.

While 'Tank' was in a coma, I phoned the CID officer in charge of the case, Superintendent Fletcher Catchpole, with regard to the condition of McGuinness. I was told he was most unwell and that it was thought that he might die. I asked Catchpole to advise me at once if he recovered consciousness, as it was my intention to see him on what could possibly be his death-bed.

I felt that if 'Tank' knew that he was dying he might well make a death-bed confession which would clear Meehan.

Several days later—but before McGuinness died—I was asked to call at Eastern police headquarters where another of my clients, John 'Gypsy' Winning, was being questioned about the McGuinness incident. Everyone knew how inseparable the two were, and had been throughout their lives. I formed the view that the questioning would be a mere formality. Winning was the last person to be seen with 'Tank' before his death.

After about an hour Winning was released and left the station with me. He had given a statement professing complete innocence. The clothing worn by Winning on the night of the injuries to McGuinness was seized by the police. In particular, his car coat was despatched for forensic examination. Now, having been questioned about his car coat, Winning would need me again.

McGuinness died on 25 March 1976—and Winning was later charged with his murder.

Winning had long been McGuinness's closest friend and I had first defended him in 1958 when I was a duty lawyer. At that time he had escaped from a prison bus on its way from Perth Prison to Barlinnie Prison in Glasgow.

Unlike his friend 'Tank', 'Gypsy' Winning was a strong, powerful man, about six feet tall. He had a Romany look about him, with long, very dark hair and striking brown eyes. Yes, 'Gypsy' would stand out in a crowd.

I recall that, then, in a plea of guilty on behalf of Winning, I described his escape as a 'fairy tale escape'—because it happened after another prisoner had run from the stationary bus, a few minutes before my client had made his move. The prison officers went after the escaping prisoner and left Winning more or less abandoned in the vehicle, with the door lying open. This allowed Winning time to think about it—and then, temptation being too much, deciding that he would also effect his escape. The circumstances were truly remarkable and I thought that my client could be excused for not looking a gift horse in the mouth.

I believe it was Winning who later recommended me to his friend 'Tank' when he required a lawyer in connection with a series of assaults and housebreakings in Kilmarnock.

Some time after this 'Tank' and 'Gypsy' made an ingenious escape from Barlinnie and, while on the run, and during the ensuing manhunt, a Dalry bank was broken into and some £25,000 stolen. Such was the expertise of the job that the blown safe was not discovered until bank employees reported for duty on the Monday morning.

On the recapture of McGuinness and Winning both stood trial at Glasgow High Court on charges of escaping from prison and with breaking into the Dalry bank. Each pled guilty to prison-breaking— but went to trial on the bank charges. 'Tank' was acquitted, and 'Gypsy' picked up a prison sentence for resetting some £4,000 of the bank proceeds, although cleared of the robbery itself. Both were sentenced to nine months for prison breaking.

They seemed to be more than satisfied with the outcome—because at Christmas that year, 1962, I received a plain card bearing a Peterhead postmark and signed simply, 'Tank and Gypsy'. This was to be the only card I have ever received from prison and it had pride of place on my mantelpiece.

On Saturday, 20 March—five days before McGuinness died—my wife, Delia, and I decided to have dinner in The Carousel restaurant in Motherwell, at that time owned by a friend of mine, Gerry Gallen. The big attraction there, for me at any rate, was the cabaret singer and pianist, John Docherty, known as 'Doc'.

Late on in the evening Delia excused herself and went to the powder room, leaving me alone at the table. Less than a minute later one of the doormen approached my table. I recognised his voice from somewhere as he said, 'Hello' to me. 'Are you still interested in Paddy Meehan?' he whispered.

My mind flashed back to similar words spoken by McGuinness in my car outside the Anvil almost three and a half years earlier. 'Of course I am,' I said.

'In that case, how would you like to have Rachel Ross's gold watch?'

'Do you have it?' I asked. I wondered if this would be another red herring by a man trying to impress.

'I can get it,' he said, 'but I cannot give the name of the man who has it.'

'I would very much like to have the watch,' was my reply. 'Can you bring it to my office on Monday?'

'Okay,' he said, 'I will do that if it will help Paddy.'

By this time my wife was returning to the table, so he withdrew, almost as stealthily as he had appeared. I discussed this most recent development with my wife before we left.

As half-expected, on Monday he did not turn up. By this time I had remembered the doorman's name as Higgins, from bygone days. It was the next afternoon, at about 4 p.m., that my receptionist told me that John Docherty (the 'Doc') was anxious to see me. He was shown into my room—I knew him quite well—and he handed me a white unsealed envelope.

Within the envelope I was quick to see a lady's gold watch, wrapped in cotton wool. This watch was to be the catalyst, as we will see . . . .

John told me that the doorman, knowing that John was coming into town on the Tuesday, had asked him to deliver this to me. I examined the expensive gold watch and noted the hallmark. I remember wishing it could speak to me. I gave John a receipt for it, after which he left. I sent for my three partners and told them of this astonishing revelation.

In their presence I telephoned the Chief Constable, to find that he was not available. I did, however, speak to an old friend of mine, Elphie Dalgleish, an Assistant Chief. I told him of this development and arranged to call at Glasgow Police Headquarters in Pitt Street at 5 p.m. that same day, with the watch.

I phoned my colleague, Len Murray, and appraised him of this development and he agreed to accompany me to the police headquarters. I remember telling Len *en route* that this might be the major breakthrough. I also told him that there might be another . . . .

Len and I met the Assistant Chief Constable and I handed over the watch and gave him a full statement outlining the events at the Carousel and the circumstances of the watch coming into my possession. I named Docherty and Higgins. I was promised that two senior CID officers—quite independent—would be instructed to investigate this new development and that they would report back to me! Satisfied, we left.

After a quick bite I went to the Faculty of Procurators' Hall in St George's Place (now Nelson Mandela Place) where I had been booked to address the Juridicial Society. I felt it difficult to control my excitement and remember saying to the assembled group of lawyers present, 'This afternoon has been noteworthy in the fight for justice in Meehan's case.' I discussed the earlier Swanson case—the first Royal

Pardon in Scotland this century on a matter of substantive crime—and told them that, as matters now looked, the second Royal Pardon might well be on the cards.

Two days later Assistant Chief Constable Arthur Bell and Detective Superintendent John MacDougall, called at my office. I knew both of them very well, having crossed swords with them on many occasions. They told me that they had been seconded to the watch enquiry, to the total exclusion of their other duties.

They said that they had already been in touch with persons in London, in an effort to check the last seven years of the watch's life. MacDougall did most of the talking and told me he had grave doubts as to the authenticity of the gold watch. He doubted that the item had ever belonged to Rachel Ross.

My heart sank yet once more—another setback.

MacDougall went on to say he was firmly of the belief that Meehan was guilty: 'I've known him for years—a cunning fox who never owns up to the commission of any of his crimes.' He went on, 'It's par for the course for Paddy to shout his innocence from the rooftops in the hope that some mug will listen.'

Bell clearly shared his view at that time, and, when they left, after half an hour, I was tempted to phone the Chief Constable to tell him that I was not too happy with his choice of 'independent' senior investigators. I did not telephone. I wrote to the Crown agent, instead, indicating that I was disappointed in the attitude of the two investigating officers.

But how wrong my initial impression proved to be! These two officers, Bell and MacDougall, were to perform their difficult task with dedication and the utmost integrity. I could not have made a better choice myself. Meehan owes them a great deal.

18

The next day the enveloping gloom evaporated in a flash. I received a telephone call from one of my police friends who said simply, 'Bill McGuinness died today in hospital.'

I telephoned Superintendent Catchpole at once for confirmation. I asked him if at any time since his admission to hospital he had recovered consciousness. He replied that he had not and that he had passed away quietly.

Between 22 and 25 March I had read with interest several newspaper reports stating that McGuinness had (a) written out a revealing statement which would shed light on the Meehan case, and (b) had made a death-bed confession to someone after recovering consciousness temporarily in the Royal Infirmary. Superintendent Catchpole confirmed that (b) was quite untrue. So far as (a), he was not at all sure as to the position here.

I left my office and went to a nearby cafeteria where I had a coffee and mulled over this latest development. Could I now go forward to the CID and divulge the contents of my many meetings with the dead man? I asked myself.

I gave thought to the mechanics of the situation. I felt that Meehan's freedom now lay in my hands—the situation was so vitally important to Meehan that I dare not err in whatever way I proposed to go about matters. Undecided as to the next course of action, I returned to my office and left it finally for the day at about 6 p.m.

I decided to go to the 'O' Sole Mio' restaurant in Bath Street which is owned by a friend of mine, Mario Romano. Very often I eat there in the evening before going home. I telephoned my wife Delia from there to tell her where I would be eating so that contact could be made with me in the event of an emergency—such as an important call to my home. This is a practice which I invariably adopt. I had a premonition, I suppose, that something big was looming on the horizon.

As I started my meal at the 'O' Sole Mio', I thought that, as a matter of courtesy, I should communicate with 'Tank's' widow before requesting the attendance of the police. This, however, could hardly be done that day—after all, it was the day of his death. I had met Mrs McGuinness on a few occasions in the past when she had accompanied her husband to the office (although she had never been present during our many Meehan talks).

At about 7.30 p.m. the restaurant telephone rang and a waiter told me that my wife requested me. I sensed that her call must relate to an important matter, otherwise she would not disturb me. I hurried to the phone and my wife told me that Owen McGuinness, 'Tank's' son, had telephoned my home.

'What did he say?' I asked.

'He said that he wanted to speak to you urgently about a document you have, written out by his father.'

Delia had told him that she would ensure that I would telephone him as soon as I returned home. She took his number. I finished my meal, and rushed home to Bothwell. I telephoned Owen McGuinness.

I extended my sympathy in respect of his father's death—'Tank' McGuinness had been, after all, a good client of mine and had a number of likeable qualities—he was by no means all bad. (I still remembered the Christmas card from Peterhead Prison sent many years earlier.)

I asked Owen why he had telephoned, and was told that his mother and he would like to see the document which his father had left with me—'To be opened after his death'. I did some quick thinking and remembered the recent newspaper items I had read. I asked Owen to call to see me next day at my office, together with his mother—and made an appointment for 3 p.m.

I had, of course, never been given such a document by 'Tank', but it was obvious to me that 'Tank's' family believed in its existence and had assumed that a letter of such importance and secrecy would be left with someone in whom they knew he had implicit trust—me. But I did not tell Owen on the phone that I was not the possessor of such a document.

After the call, I appraised my wife of the dramatic turn of events, and told her about the significance of 'Tank's' death, *vis à vis* Meehan's now more sanguine prospects. Much would also depend on the McGuinness family whom I had arranged to meet on the following afternoon.

On the dot of 3 p.m. Agnes McGuinness, her son, Owen, and his sister arrived at my office. Within seconds all three were seated in front of me at my desk. Mrs McGuinness asked me if I had a sealed envelope given to me by her late husband. An envelope, she said, which related to the case of Paddy Meehan.

I told her that I did not have this, nor had I seen such an envelope, although I had read something about it in the Press recently. All three seemed surprised, and told me that, months earlier, 'Tank' had told them in confidence that he had written out an exhaustive account of his involvement in the Ayr murder, that he had placed it in an envelope, sealed it, and marked it, 'To be opened only in the event of my death'.

They went on to say that he had told them that he had left it in the safest of hands. These hands, they assumed, must be mine.

I told them that he had seen me often over the past three years about Meehan's case, that he had been troubled about it, and that he had done his best to assist Meehan, short of being charged himself. To my surprise they knew all about our meetings. Mrs McGuinness then told me it had been her late husband's wish for her to end Meehan's agony, particularly following his death.

From the way they talked, it appeared that for some considerable time he felt that death was not very far away. It was crystal clear that all three of them knew full well of Meehan's innocence, and 'Tank's' involvement with someone other than Meehan or Griffiths in the Ayr affair. Mrs McGuinness named the second man as Ian Waddell.

They were also clear in their intention to go forward to the authorities, in order to assist in the clarification of the whole matter of this bizarre murder saga.

You can imagine my excitement (although I tried not to show it) ... we were nearing the end of a long, tortuous road. This must surely be the countdown to the inevitable Royal Pardon—I was no longer wasting my time, tilting at windmills.

I told them that I planned to give the police a full statement in the near future, in view of the fact that I felt that my confidentiality pledge had ceased to exist, consequent upon my client's death.

To their credit, they were in entire agreement with me. I told them that I proposed to take up the matter of confidentiality with the Law Society—after all, this situation was unique and totally without precedent.

I followed this up by asking them, as my late client's next-of-kin, if they would be agreeable to sign Minutes of Waiver in which it would be narrated that each one of them (widow, son and daughter) waived the issue of confidentiality, and requested that I hand over to the authorities all details of the McGuinness-Beltrami meetings about Meehan, in the interest and pursuit of justice.

They were, indeed, unanimous about this, and I arranged that they should call next morning to sign the Minutes, which I would, in the meantime, have drawn up.

On Saturday, 27 March, all three kept their appointment with me and the Minutes of Waiver of confidentiality by the next of kin were duly signed and witnessed by two of my staff. I put them away in my file and supplied them with copies, thanking them profusely for their forthrightness.

I could well understand why they did not come forward to me during 'Tank's' lifetime—blood, as they say, is thicker than water. To their credit, they had wasted little time after his death.

I proceeded to take from each of them (one at a time and outwith the presence of the others) detailed statements relating to the Ayr case, and realised that Mrs McGuinness knew about her husband's involvement within days of the murder, and before Meehan's arrest. Later, her son and daughter found out about it, too, to their eternal sorrow.

I was given information about which even I was unaware . . . the jigsaw pieces were now fitting into place—and rapidly at that.

In particular, Mrs McGuinness told me that her husband had told her about being stopped by 'the busies' in Racecourse Road, close to the Ross bungalow early in the morning *and being driven in a police Panda car to the Ayr bus depot.* She told how he had doubled back and had deposited the Ross car keys and the two lady's rings *en route.* Now I realised the significance of the rough sketch drawn when he was trying to help me trace the drains—and why he had started his sketch at the Ayr bus depot.

Having taken the three helpful and revealing, not to say sensational, statements in longhand, I talked to them about the mysterious sealed envelope containing the confession. This would be excellent evidence, were I able to obtain it. He would hardly have lied to his family about this matter, having been so frank with them about the other facts.

'And it's in the hands of a trusted person,' I mused. . . .

I thought of his great friend, John 'Gypsy' Winning, who would later be questioned by the police about 'Tank's' death. Later, I questioned Winning about this sealed document, but he was not aware of its existence.

I remembered his Shettleston bank and told Mrs McGuinness that I would have the manager seen on the Monday.

I knew that McGuinness had been a Catholic (non-practising at that time) and ascertained from her the name of the local Roman Catholic Church, and that of the parish priest. She confirmed that he had not attended a mass for many years—but I thought, once a Catholic . . . .

I also took from her the name of his doctor, and remembered that he had seen a psychiatrist in the previous year. She could not tell me the psychiatrist's name or address, so I asked her to go home and make a thorough search of the house in the hope that she might find an appointment card there. Extremely co-operative, as she had been the previous day, she promised to do this and made an appointment to see me on the following Monday.

Next day was a Sunday and a rest day—but don't you believe it!

I thought about the course of action that would have to be taken. The Crown could not possibly ignore this dramatic turn of events—it must lead to Meehan's release.

I thought of Oscar Slater, who, in 1927, had his conviction for murder quashed in the Court of Criminal Appeal, Edinburgh. New evidence had been led on his behalf, and that some 18 years after his conviction and sentence.

Alternatively, had not another of my clients, Maurice Swanson, received the Royal Pardon in the previous year (26 July 1975) as a result of having gone through the Executive channels, by-passing the Judiciary? Had not Swanson been properly compensated, too, for his wrongful incarceration over a period of 11 months—and that to the extent of £5,000? Having been completely successful in the Swanson tactics and procedures, I opted for the 'devil I knew'.

Frankly, I felt that some Lords Commissioners of Justiciary were not, and never had been, kindly disposed to Meehan's position. My view was aptly justified at the trial of Ian Waddell in respect of the same Ayr murder, later that year. Lord Robertson, the Trial Judge then, made his feelings about Meehan's pardon—the first on a murder charge in Scotland this century—crystal clear, as will emerge later. He was firmly of the view that Meehan should not have been pardoned, far less compensated for his lengthy prison sojourn.

Lawyers (whether they be judges or lesser mortals) have been only too ready to apply the whitewash brush to possible miscarriages of justice, instead of the microscope.

Slow to pursue the most blatant errors by the crime investigators, or the trial judges, some seem determined not to 'rock the establishment boat' and pretend to have an infallible and omniscient legal system, incapable of succumbing to human error or frailty.

In all conscience, such persons can't believe this to be the case, but spend their lives in the pretence that it is. Alternatively, they are prepared to hide behind the verdict of a jury on the basis that such 'privileged' persons as a group, can do no wrong and so enjoy a 'divine' right to arrive at the correct conclusion by drawing wholly unimpeachable inferences.

In short, the golden thread that runs through justice can become somewhat tarnished.

19

Two Royal Pardons in Scotland this century clearly indicate the immense and almost insurmountable difficulties in righting judicial wrong. I know a number of persons serving lengthy sentences who are victims of jury errors. The distance between this state of affairs and a Royal Pardon is monumental in its vastness.

I took the crucial decision that same Sunday—it must be done through the Executive, the Secretary of State for Scotland, as in Swanson's case. On the Monday, I briefed my office manager, Michael MacDonald, of all recent developments and asked him to go to the Shettleston bank at once, in order to find out if the manager had the document—or if 'Tank' had a safety deposit box there.

On the previous evening, I had dinner with my own curate, Father H. Alison, along with the parish priest of Craigend, which is close to what would have been 'Tank's' parish in Garthamlock. I knew Father McColgan of Craigend very well—he having earlier been a curate in Bothwell. I explained the matter to them, and Father McColgan agreed to speak to his clerical neighbour about the document. He also agreed to telephone me on the following evening. This he did—but we drew another blank.

Mrs McGuinness kept her appointment and produced a psychiatrist's appointment card which she had found, with difficulty, at her home in Milncroft Road. I thanked her and told her that I would be in touch again very soon.

Mr MacDonald duly returned. There was no safety deposit box, nor had the manager been given an envelope by McGuinness. He did ascertain, however, that McGuinness had lodged a substantial sum of money in his account fairly soon after the date of the Ayr murder. This was further confirmation of the information 'Tank' had given me some time earlier—I remembered his annoyance at his own stupidity in doing this.

Michael MacDonald was then despatched to the psychiatrist's clinic in Woodside, armed with the appointment card. He drew another blank—no envelope. He did, however, take a useful statement from the psychiatrist who spoke about 'Tank's' fears for his own safety, and his concern about a 'material matter' (although the psychiatrist was never given details about this material matter). He did know that it concerned someone outside his family.

On 26 and 29 March and again on 5 April 1976, I wrote to the Secretary of the Law Society—R. B. Laurie. I explained as much of my problem as I could. I told him about Meehan and McGuinness, both clients, and of 'Tank's' confessions to me. I explained that I wished to go to the police as soon as possible, and that I was now sure that I could secure Meehan's release. I emphasised the urgency of the matter and enclosed all three Minutes of Waiver, signed by the next-of-kin. After this, I prepared my statement which I proposed to give to the police, and put it in my ever-growing file of papers.

Two weeks later I telephoned Mr Wheelan, the President of the Law Society of Scotland at that time, asked him what was happening about my letters, and pointed out that every day counted so far as Meehan was concerned.

The President could not give me a decision but suggested I should write to the Dean of the Faculty of Advocates, for his opinion on the matter. I retorted that I was not a member of the Faculty of Advocates, but of the Law Society of Scotland, of which he was the President. In any event, if the Dean of the Faculty of Advocates had said 'No', I would have proceeded against his advice. Indeed, if the Law Society had ruled against me I doubt if I could have stopped myself—the momentum was now so considerable.

My Society, as I thought, was merely sitting on the fence. I gave notice to the President there and then that I intended to telephone Assistant Chief Constable Arthur Bell, at once, and this I promptly did.

Even to this day I have not received a proper answer to the letters sent by me to the Secretary of the Law Society of Scotland.

Bell arranged to call on me, with Chief Superintendent John MacDougall, on Monday 12 April. When they came, I gave him a full and detailed statement. I told them about the statements of the McGuinness family and suggested that they should be seen at once.

I know that after seeing the McGuinness family the two senior officers swung considerably to my side.

Several days earlier I had phoned Ludo, outlined the recent developments, and a committee meeting was arranged for Sunday 11 April at the Station Hotel in Perth.

For days before this, I realised the news media knew that something was in the air concerning Meehan. I was bombarded with telephone calls from our many national newspapers, even the *Sunday Times*. I told them absolutely nothing—the matter was far too delicate and required to be handled with the utmost tact.

At the Perth committee meeting there was a full attendance both of members of the Press (outside) and those of the Committee. I had already advised Mrs Meehan and her son, Pat, of some of the happenings—but not all. They asked to attend the meeting, but I felt it best that they didn't.

I had my file of papers at the meeting—with the various, recently-gathered statements—and copies of the Minutes of Waiver and my copy letters to the Law Society of Scotland.

This was to be one of the few occasions when Ludo and I disagreed.

The meeting started with my giving the members an outline of the recent developments. Ludo wanted to advise the waiting Pressmen of everything and so, as he thought, force the authorities to act.

Embarrass them, might be the operative words.

I had anticipated such a schism and had taken the precaution, in advance of the meeting, of conferring with the committee member closest to me in the many developments—Glasgow lawyer Len Murray—outside the Glasgow Sheriff Court early that same morning. I had driven Len to Perth and *en route* had shown him the McGuinness statements, as well as the other precognitions.

I had discussed the matter fully with Len. I had always had the utmost respect for his tactical powers and his intelligent reading of difficult situations, based on his considerable experience over many years. Len and I had been in many cases together, and, between us, have seldom, I think, made an incorrect or hasty decision.

I told Len of my fears of the forthcoming committee meeting—that the matter should not be splashed to the general public at this stage, and we *must* give the Executive unhampered and unfettered powers to act in privacy. In short, we must give the Crown Office (and Mr Chalmers, in particular) its right and proper place.

Len took the point, as I knew he would. I knew that he would support me in the event of the inevitable clash between myself and other members of the committee. That being so, you may wonder why I was so anxious to have the meeting convened in the first place.

I was a member of this committee (a founder member) and felt that it would be unfair were I to proceed to correspond with the Crown Agent without the sanction of the committee. In any event, seven heads are, and always were, better than one.

But I disagreed very strongly with Ludo as to our next step. Unlike Ludo, I had the utmost confidence in Bill Chalmers, the Crown Agent, and felt that, given the new developments, he would most certainly act, and act swiftly and fairly.

The situation became somewhat heated, and Ludo suggested a vote—I countered by saying that this would be pointless as I had no intention of reading out the statements which I had, were they to be made public that day. I would simply resign from the committee and pursue the matter myself. Alternatively, I intimated that I was prepared to take over the chair.

Len steadfastly supported me from the outset—others sided with Ludo. I emphasised that we were now so near to complete victory, and stated that it would be unfortunate if the committee were split. If I resigned, I said that my papers would go with me, leaving the committee little by way of bargaining power.

After much discussion, we reached an agreement. I would be in early communication with the Crown Agent and the police (next day), and if there were to be unsatisfactory progress I would agree to public statements by the committee within, say, three weeks. I promised to report back to them as soon as possible, through the chairman.

Thereafter, a very non-committal and somewhat terse statement was drafted for the eager Pressmen. They were told of the possibility of monumental moves—but no details—and staggering results within a period of two months.

I was to meet Bell and MacDougall on not a few occasions. Over the ensuing weeks, they often phoned me at home and, excitedly, told me of developments—all good. They were clearly impressed by the statements given by the McGuinness family. They were now as convinced as I was in respect of Meehan's innocence. I sincerely hope they were more than satisfied with my own detailed statement as to 'Tank's' admissions to me.

They checked the car-hire firm in Edinburgh (Carnie's) and confirmed the signature of McGuinness. They confirmed the bank lodgement shortly after the robbery. They confirmed that his daughter Elizabeth had been in Irvine on the fateful weekend. Everything now fitted into place like a gigantic jigsaw. The conclusion was inevitable.

By now, there was a torrent of incontrovertible evidence clearing Meehan.

That same day I sent copies of everything to the Crown Agent with a lengthy covering letter, wherein I touched upon the difficulties experienced on the previous day at Perth, and the fact that the Press and television had not been made conversant with the up-to-date situation.

Matters moved fast. Bill Chalmers, the Crown Agent, personally precognosced the relevant witnesses (including one in Perth Prison, who had written to me stating that he would assist Meehan in his fight for justice). Another prisoner in Peterhead had written to me concerning a meeting he had had with Waddell in Manchester. Waddell had spoken of his involvement and I had made arrangements to travel to Peterhead. The Crown Agent did this for me. Chalmers was most ably backed by Bell and MacDougall, who set about their task with zeal and great skill.

In addition to checking the Shettleston Bank and Carnie's Car-Hire in Edinburgh, they checked additional medical evidence about a breast operation carried out on Rachel Ross some little time before the murder and referred to by 'Tank'; the two police officers who had picked him up in the early hours of the morning and had driven him to the bus station in Ayr (they found their original statements); and the fact that Abraham Ross's car keys had mysteriously disappeared that night. The officers saw the psychiatrist, and they managed to 'break' the alibi supplied to Waddell by courtesy of Mr and Mrs Donald Carmichael. They also discovered that Waddell (then unemployed) had been in possession of substantial funds shortly after the Ayr murder, and had used an East End publican as his banker.

By 26 April they were back in my office and brought me up to date with their extensive enquiries. They, too, were excited whereas they are normally fairly phlegmatic in their approach. What a turnaround! In late March they were entirely hostile to my pleas—now they were totally convinced that Meehan was innocent, that the crime had been committed by McGuinness and Waddell. The pieces now fitted together and a completed picture had emerged. I was elated to have won over these two experienced officers, who had earlier been so derisory about even the remotest possibility of Meehan's innocence.

They told me that they would be travelling to Edinburgh soon to report finally to the Lord Advocate, Ronald King Murray (now Lord Murray, Senator of the College of Justice). They would also report to the Solicitor General at that time, John McCluskey (now Lord McCluskey) and Bill Chalmers, Crown Agent.

20

My next move was to write to the Crown Agent in Edinburgh to say that 'in the very name of justice' Meehan must now be pardoned.

A few days later, in early May, John MacDougall telephoned me at home in the late evening to tell me (unofficially, of course) that Meehan would soon receive the Queen's Pardon, and that this fact would be announced in the House of Commons by the Lord Advocate or Scottish Secretary.

This was music to my ears—my eyes filled. I thanked him profusely, and immediately telephoned my partner, Douglas Forbes. He was still sceptical, and thought that I was exaggerating just a little. 'We'll wait and see,' was his firm attitude.

Two days later mention was made of the case in Parliament and the Lord Advocate stated that he would make a statement in the House on 19 May. In the back of my mind I thought that if the statement were unfavourable and indefinite all would be irretrievably lost—if they were not satisfied by now, the position would be, as it had always seemed, impossible.

The Press calls became more numerous, and I allowed myself at last to say that Meehan should be released sometime in May. This was, of course, headline news—I hoped that I would not appear to be too presumptuous. I felt that I could rely unflinchingly on John Mac-Dougall's information. I also kept Ludo in touch and prepared for the now inevitable release of Patrick Meehan.

Weeks earlier I had urged the McGuinness family to make no statements to the Press under any circumstances—I knew that the

Press would get around to trying. Dutifully, they responded to my instruction and the Crown Agent was allowed to proceed with his monumental task without interruption. In short, I wanted the Crown to take full credit for the now imminent pardon, although it must later emerge that I had triggered off the mechanism for it.

The Crown did not let me (or my committee) down. At about 3 p.m. on the afternoon of Wednesday 19 May I received a telephone call from St Andrew's House while I was at the High Court in Glasgow. Their representative advised me, as I had earlier been advised in Swanson's case, that at 4 p.m. the Scottish Secretary (then Bruce Millan) would announce in Parliament that Meehan would be granted a Royal Pardon and would be released from Peterhead that very moment.

What a feeling that was—the impossible had taken place.

Sure enough, at 4 p.m. a statement was made. This is an extract from Parliament's *Hansard*:

Patrick Meehan.

  Secretary of State for Scotland (Bruce Millan):

  As the House knows, I have been considering the case of Patrick Meehan. Patrick Meehan was charged with the murder of Mrs Abraham Ross at Ayr, and on 24th October 1969, in the High Court of Justiciary in Edinburgh, was convicted of the murder and sentenced to Life Imprisonment.

  He appealed against his conviction to the Court of Criminal Appeal, and, after a hearing, his appeal was dismissed on 25th November, 1969.

  Since that time there have been representations regarding the conviction to successive Secretaries of State for Scotland based on the case against Mr Meehan at the trial, but also on other matters, including statements by another man alleging his participation in the robbery and murder.

  In the last few days I have received new information following the death of William McGuinness, a man with a record of crimes of dishonesty and violence. It was revealed after his death that he had made statements to the effect that he had participated in the Ross robbery to the exclusion of Mr Meehan.

  The value of these statements must remain a matter of judgment, but there is independent evidence establishing that Mr McGuinness was in Ayr on the night of the murder. I have considered whether the case might again be brought under judicial review.

  The only provision of law by which a conviction, once reached and appealed against, can be restored to the judicial field is my power to refer a case back under section 63 (1A) of the Criminal Procedure (Scotland) Act 1975.

However, by statute, the Court could not go wider in considering the case than it can in an ordinary appeal against conviction, and, having regard to the nature of the considerations relevant to a decision of the case, I have reached the conclusion that my powers of reference back are inappropriate to it.

Nor would further investigation or enquiry be likely to lead to the discovery of such further information as to make such a reference appropriate.

In the circumstances I have reached a conclusion that it falls to me as Secretary of State to reach a decision of whether or not to recommend the exercise of the Royal Prerogative on the new information which has become available since the death of McGuinness.

I have therefore decided to recommend the exercise of the Royal Prerogative to grant a Free Pardon. Mr Meehan is being released today.

My Right Honourable and learned friend the Lord Advocate is at present considering in light of the new evidence, whether he should instruct any further investigations with a view to possible criminal proceedings.

On his release, Meehan was spirited away by a national newspaper and for several days his explosive story covered the main pages of the *Daily Record* and then the *Sunday Mail*.

At four-thirty on the afternoon of 19 May, Mrs Betty Meehan had telephoned me from Peterhead to thank me.

Thereafter the Press, as always, linked the 'Tank's' killing to Meehan's position, and there were headlines such as, 'Who Killed McGuinness—Meehan's friends?', 'Was "Tank" killed to force the Meehan issue?' For my part, I felt, and still feel, that there was absolutely no connection whatsoever between the death of McGuinness and Meehan.

Our chairman, Ludo, wrote an article in the *News of the World* in which he stated—on what basis I know not—'I believe McGuinness was killed to free Meehan. The underworld killed the real Ayr murderer. It was only after his slaying that his solicitor, J. Beltrami, was freed from his professional code of silence.'

I was quoted as saying that 'in my view' McGuinness had been the victim of a drunken brawl, his death being entirely coincidental so far as Meehan was concerned. That is still my opinion.

Another committee meeting was arranged at the North British Hotel in Edinburgh. The idea was to discuss the important question of compensation for Meehan. Prior to this I had issued a statement to the Press that, following upon Meehan's pardon, I had been in communication with the Crown Agent and the Lord Advocate requesting a formal pardon for the deceased James Griffiths.

At the meeting, David Burnside, an Aberdeen solicitor (now heavily involved in the Piper Alpha case) advised me that he was pursuing the matter of compensation so I allowed him to look at my Swanson file which I had taken to the meeting.

My own view was that the committee should pursue the compensation aspect (it had only happened once before in our lifetime, and that was the previous year in my Swanson case), and I felt that my background knowledge would be valuable. Indeed, I would have been happy to follow up the quest myself, as I had done all the correspondence after 'Tank's' death. It was in 1982 that Meehan asked me to take over his claim personally. I agreed on the spot.

At the time of this final committee meeting, I was about to have my hands full anyway, because on a Friday in June 1976, after the Royal Pardon euphoria, John 'Gypsy' Winning was arrested in a Gallowgate public house and charged with the murder of McGuinness, his best friend.

I was telephoned by the police and went to see him at once. I discovered that Detective Superintendent Catchpole was on holiday, otherwise I am sure that he would have arranged with me to bring Winning in voluntarily, rather than to have him arrested in an East End public house. The officer in charge of the case (in the absence of Catchpole) had not appreciated the arrangement arrived at between Catchpole and myself. To say that Winning was surprised at his arrest would be an understatement—he was utterly astonished.

On being charged at the police bar, he had vehemently denied the matter. I saw him at the Eastern Police Headquarters and arranged to appear for him the next day at Glasgow Sheriff Court. I duly represented him at the Court, when he formally appeared on petition on the following charge:

John Winning, of no fixed abode, you are charged that you did on 12th March 1976, in Janefield Street at Springfield Road, Glasgow, assault William McGuinness of 26 Milncroft Road, Glasgow, knock him to the ground and kick him repeatedly in the head and face to his severe injury, in consequence whereof he died on 25th March, 1976, at Glasgow Royal Infirmary, and you did murder him.

No plea or declaration was made by him, and he was remanded in custody for further enquiries by Sheriff Francis Middleton.

Winning's statement to me was that he and 'Tank' had been drinking in 'Tank's' brother-in-law's house in Waddell Court, Glasgow. The brother-in-law had driven both of them in his car to the junction of London Road/Springfield Road, when both had left and proceeded to walk along Springfield Road. 'Both,' said the brother-in-law, Francis O'Brien, 'were tipsy, but they were always friendly.'

Winning told me that they had split up in Springfield Road and that he (Winning) went off to the house of a friend nearby, in order to spend the night there, as he felt just a little sick. He had found out about 'Tank's' injuries sometime next day.

I know that the police knew all this when they released him in March, after questioning, and gathered that further evidence must have come to light after the forensic examination of Winning's clothing.

Sure enough, three days after his initial court appearance, I was telephoned by Superintendent Catchpole. He had been instructed to have a sample of blood taken from my client in the prison. Mr Catchpole also apologised to me for not arranging the arrest of Winning through me, but pointed out that he had been on holiday at the time when the warrant had come through. Normally, in the case of a suspect having been interviewed with his solicitor present, then released, if new developments meant further action by the police then the solicitor would be asked by the police to make himself and his client available at the police station. Had Catchpole not been on holiday, he could merely have telephoned me to say that he had an arrest warrant for Winning. A suitable time would then have been arranged and Winning and I would have called to see him.

I told Mr Catchpole that I would not agree to the blood sample being taken from Winning, and that he should report that fact back to the Procurator Fiscal, who would then apply to the sheriff for a warrant ordering the accused to give a sample of his blood. I asked him to advise the Fiscal that I wished to argue the matter before the sheriff, and so would require notice of the application.

Two days later, the Fiscal and I appeared before Sheriff Marcus Stone in Glasgow. The matter took some two hours to resolve—

previous cases (and there were not many) and principles were argued and distinguished and the liberty of the subject canvassed—but, eventually, Sheriff Stone granted the much-sought-after warrant to take my client's blood sample.

Next day, I met Catchpole and another police officer at the prison, having previously interviewed my client and told him that he must not object to the taking of blood.

Winning, as always, accepted my advice. Despite all the trouble in obtaining the warrant, I was surprised that Catchpole, as he explained, turned up at the prison without the proper label for the blood phial. I thought little of this at the time—but it was unusual, and the charge was, after all, the most serious in our criminal calendar. The sample was duly taken by a prison doctor and the two CID officers and I left the prison.

Only one CID officer lodged the sample taken from Winning at Pitt Street's forensic laboratory. The sample was put in a refrigerator (after 6 p.m.) at a time when no one else was present there. Accordingly, it was not officially booked in by a second person – and the label was flawed in any event.

The High Court pleading diet was set for 6 August, 1976, the trial for 16 August. The charge remained the same as has been earlier described, and the trial was to take place before the Lord Justice Clerk, the Rt. Hon. Lord Wheatley.

In the course of my preparations I discovered what the additional evidence was which caused the re-arrest of Winning. On his car coat the forensic experts had found traces of human blood. This blood had been analysed and was found to consist of a most unusual group. So unusual was this group, that only a tiny percentage of Glasgow's population shared it. The percentage was 0.38 of one per cent.

The blood sample taken from Winning showed that his blood group was much more common. The sample from the car coat (shades of James Griffiths, yet another coincidence) had been compared with the sample of 'Tank's' blood allegedly taken at the post mortem examination by Professor Harland. It matched in every detail.

The Crown would thus seek to establish that Winning was the last person seen with McGuinness—and only 15 minutes before a passer-by had discovered the unconscious figure—and that it was likely (from the rarity of his blood group) that the car coat worn by Winning that same night had traces of 'Tank's' blood. So the experts would say.

The case was not an easy one, although there would, I felt, have been insufficient evidence to convict without the blood findings.

The two-day trial proceeded on the appointed date. Evidence was led by the Crown to the effect that Winning and McGuinness had left O'Brien's house and had been driven by him to London Road at Springfield Road. O'Brien stated that there were no arguments in the car and that they were, as always, friendly, although drunk. O'Brien went on to say that Winning was wearing a car coat and identified the relevant Crown label production.

No motive emerged in respect of the murder. O'Brien dropped both of them off, and, when last seen by him, they were walking along Springfield Road in a normal manner. O'Brien then drove back to his Waddell Court home.

Evidence was led by the Crown that a phial of blood, alleged to have been scooped from McGuinness's stomach at the post mortem by Professor Harland, contained a rare blood group. The same type of blood was found on Winning's car coat, it was claimed.

There was, however, conflicting evidence as to whether or not a blood sample had been taken from the body of McGuinness at the post mortem examination in the City Mortuary. One pathologist who was present stated that he could not remember if a blood sample had been taken, while another said a blood sample had definitely not been taken. Two senior police officers who had been present were adamant that it had been taken.

There was, then, a looseness and slackness surrounding *each* blood sample, which fell short of the standard of proof required by our courts—that is, proof beyond reasonable doubt. The additional evidence bringing about Winning's re-arrest was therefore suspect in law, and we decided not to call Winning to explain the blood-staining on his car coat. Winning accepted our advice.

We did call, however, a defence witness, James Bruce, who said that in February that same year he had been drinking in the Braemar Bar in London Road, Glasgow, when McGuinness and Winning had come into the premises on their way to a mid-week, floodlit soccer match at nearby Celtic Park. McGuinness took an exception to a remark that Bruce had made about Meehan's position, and had assaulted him with his fists. Winning, wearing his car coat (again shades of James Griffiths), managed to separate them. McGuinness's nose had been bleeding at the time, as Bruce had retaliated after the unexpected attack on his person.

This could have accounted for such blood being discovered on the car coat later on. McGuinness was described during the trial (by the police and other witnesses) as a violent psychopath with many enemies. He was also a man who went in fear of his life, and for weeks before his death had seldom crossed his doorstep. There could be many persons interested in killing him, but, and the police conceded this, his best friend for many years had been the accused, John 'Gypsy' Winning.

The cross examination of Bruce was of little consequence, and thereafter, we closed the case for the Defence. Lorn Cowie QC, the Advocate Depute, rose and requested an adjournment to consider the Crown's position. We did not oppose this motion, and Lord Wheatley granted it.

After the 20-minute recess, Cowie addressed Lord Wheatley as follows: 'Having heard all the evidence, in particular that relating to the possibility of blood having got on to the car coat in some other way, plus some of the difficulties in dealing with the checking of both blood samples, I am of the view that there is simply not enough evidence against John Winning, and, accordingly, I withdraw the indictment'.

I do not presume to know the reason for the 'difficulties' applicable to the respective blood samples but concede that the legal deficiencies in respect of each undoubtedly assisted the defence.

Lord Wheatley agreed that certain requisites in law had not been met, and added that if Mr Cowie had not taken this step, he would have told the jury to bring in a verdict of Not Guilty. The jury was formerly instructed to find Winning Not Guilty by the direction of the Court, and he walked free from the dock, showing no sign of emotion.

In view of the interest surrounding this trial and the link between McGuinness and Meehan a Press Conference was held in one of the small rooms within the High Court building. Winning faced reporters with me at his side, and told them that 'Tank' had always been his best friend: 'He was the sort of man I chose to escape from prison with ... you cannot ask higher than that. I know to some people he had the reputation of being a violent man ... I never saw any badness in him. He was the sort of person you could telephone up in the morning, and get fifty pounds in your hand by tea-time. We sat together in the same dock I have just left—charged with escaping from prison and robbing a bank in Dalry, Ayrshire. That was in 1962.'

Asked to explain his death, he said, 'He may have been attacked by men—men who caught up with him.'

Asked if he thought that there might have been a link with the Meehan case, he replied, 'I don't know, but I don't think so. I know nothing about the Meehan case. 'Tank' was a very proud family man—close to his wife and children. When I was released by the police, after the initial questioning, I wanted to go and see Mrs McGuinness but Mr Beltrami would not hear of that. I would like to see his widow and family now. Yes, Billy was my best pal, and I will miss him a lot.'

When Winning consulted me in my office, after his temporary release in early April, pending the outcome of the forensic scientists' study of his clothing, I asked him if he could help me in connection with Meehan. His reply was, that he would say nothing involving Billy. Although McGuinness was known as 'Tank' he always referred to him as 'Billy'.

He seemed so definite about the matter, that I decided not to pursue it. I remembered looking at Winning, and thinking to myself: 'This man could assist me greatly in clearing Meehan, but is in no way prepared to do so.'

When next I saw Winning in my office, it was on the afternoon of his acquittal, in August 1976. He came up to thank me as he obviously appreciated that the case had not been as easy as it appeared to onlookers in Court. By that time Meehan had already been pardoned, and, once again, I mentioned his name to him. Yet once more he was unprepared to betray any confidence in respect of Billy, but merely told me that he was going to look up Meehan and ask him to lend him some cash.

After this, Winning left my office. The good client that he was over many years, I was never to see again.

21

Shortly after the outcome of the Winning trial, I saw Messrs Bell and MacDougall once again in my office. A succession of questions were put to me about Meehan, and I gathered that I would soon be called upon to give evidence for the Crown in the case against Ian Waddell, who was obviously about to be charged with the 1969 Ayr murder, while acting along with 'Tank' McGuinness.

Yet another strange coincidence was that Meehan was charged while acting along with a dead man (Griffiths) and Waddell was about to be charged, while acting along with another dead man (McGuinness).

I must say, I was not happy about the prospect of Waddell being charged—I could not see a jury convicting Waddell for a crime committed seven years earlier, and a crime for which Meehan and the deceased Griffiths had already been convicted. To my knowledge, this was the first time this century that such a situation had occurred, namely, where there had been an earlier trial in which a man was convicted, and, so many years later, a further trial about the same circumstances in which another man, not tried in the first instance, was before the Court, the earlier convicted man being a Crown witness against him.

I knew, however, that there was now a considerable body of evidence against Waddell and McGuinness, as a result of the unstinting efforts of Bell and MacDougall.

Before the arraignment of Ian Waddell, yet something else was to happen. The Scottish Office nominated D. Bruce Weir QC (now Lord Weir) to assess compensation for Meehan. D. Bruce Weir is the son-in-law of Lord Cameron, the senior High Court Judge, who was on the bench of three judges who (a) rejected our truth drug application prior to the trial, and (b) turned down Meehan's appeal against conviction in late 1969.

A strange choice, I thought, as assessor.

An interim award of £2,500 was paid out to Meehan within weeks of his pardon, but sometime after that the final figure of £7,500 (which was to include £500 towards my legal expenses) was computed. Meehan, very properly and on my advice, rejected this puny offer.

Then I learned from Bell and MacDougall, in strictest confidence, that Waddell and Dick were about to be charged—Waddell with the murder and other charges, and Dick with the charge of conspiracy to murder. I said not one word about this matter to anyone in the world.

I did express the view to Messrs Bell and MacDougall that I, as an individual, was not particularly happy about the prospect of these charges being taken and that I was not at all certain that the charges would be accepted by a jury.

I did not wish a situation to arise where Meehan was virtually on trial again. After all, it was clear that Waddell in his own defence would require to impeach Meehan and Griffiths. It was patently obvious, as night follows day.

One afternoon in August, as I was walking back to my West George Street office, a police car stopped beside me and Superintendent John MacDougall put his head out. He told me that he was now in possession of the warrant for the arrest of the two men in connection with the Ayr murder, some seven years earlier.

This was surely history in the making.

Next day, sure enough, the newspapers were full of it. Waddell and Dick had been arrested and appeared that day on petition before a Sheriff in Glasgow. Robert Gibson represented Ian Waddell, J. Ross Harper appeared on behalf of Andrew Dick.

Looking at the indictment, it was clear that Messrs Bell and MacDougall had conducted a most searching and extensive enquiry. They had left no stone unturned in their determination to get to the whole truth of the matter.

Waddell, naturally, was not given bail because he faced, among other charges, one of murder. He was, in any event, serving a sentence for assault at that time.

Here was a new accused, Waddell, impeached by us earlier when we had proceeded—we had no choice—without the advantages of the developments of seven long and anxious years. Impeachment, or incrimination as it is also called, means maintaining innocence but also stating that the crime was committed by another person. Prior intimation of such a defence line must be given to the court and the prosecutor, otherwise the accused would be precluded from blaming anyone for the crime.

At the pleading diet, as I anticipated, Waddell pled alibi and impeached Griffiths and Meehan (matters had turned full circle). In addition, there were pleas to the competency and relevancy of the indictment. A debate was fixed for 5 October 1976, at Edinburgh High Court before Lord Robertson.

Out of interest, I turned up at the hearing, along with Ludo and Meehan. We intended to listen to the historic debate. Defence Counsel and the Lord Advocate agreed that, although Crown witnesses, we could attend, as this was a legal debate, but Lord Robertson ruled that we should not be present. 'Their evidence may be of great importance,' he said.

Having been told to leave the Court, all three of us went for coffee and biscuits and passed our time discussing the matter of Meehan's compensation. We tried to quantify it. Naturally, Meehan's ideas were far in excess of mine. Over coffee, Meehan, who had never really lost his acute sense of humour, remarked, 'That's the first time I have ever been turned away from a Court.'

We learned that Lord Robertson had ruled that the trial would proceed.

Perhaps it would be timely, here, to set out the exact terms of the Royal Pardon granted to Meehan—a certified copy of which still has a prominent place in my West Nile Street office in Glasgow. The Pardon is superscribed by our Queen, Elizabeth R. and is as follows:

Elizabeth the Second, by the grace of God of the United Kingdom of Great Britain and Northern Ireland and of our other realms and territories Queen, head of the Commonwealth, Defender of the Faith, to all to whom these presents shall come, greeting!

Whereas Patrick Connelly Meehan was at the High Court holden at Edinburgh, on 24th day of October, 1969 convicted of murder and sentenced to Life Imprisonment; NOW KNOW YE, that we in consideration of some circumstances humbly presented unto us and of our Prerogative Royal, proper motion, and Royal clemency are graciously pleased to extend our grace and mercy to the said Patrick Connelly

Meehan and to grant him a free Pardon in respect of the said
conviction thereby pardoning, remitting and releasing unto him all
pains, penalties and punishments whatsoever that from the said conviction may come. Given at our Court, at St. James the 19th day of May
1976, in the 25th year of our reign.
Signed: Bruce Millan
Secretary of State for Scotland.

It is worth noting that this document is identical in every way to that
of Maurice Swanson. In the latter case there was no furore—he was
properly compensated in respect of the accepted and wrongful depriva-
tion of liberty as a result of erroneous identification by two bank
tellers. In Swanson's case, the Pardon expunged the conviction completely and for all time. I agree, the terms of the Pardon are archaic
and anachronistic—the wording should surely be brought up-to-date
to conform to our normal vernacular. It is superscribed, as I have said,
by the Queen and I suppose its quaint terms stem from the fact that
the monarch 'can do no wrong'.

Correspondingly, she cannot publicly admit to error. In modern
times this simply will not do, and one hopes that in the interests of
justice and fairness to the subjects in the future, one might find a more
sensibly drawn document stating *inter alia* that, 'A gross error has
been made, as the result of which one of Her Majesty's subjects was
wrongly convicted, and that, in order to rectify matters, the said
wrongous conviction will be unequivocally expunged from the
record.'

There must surely be parity in relation to the spirit engendered by
such a rare document, if logic is to be maintained—as, in the name of
justice and equity, it must. These Royal Pardons are not, I can assure
you, easy to achieve.

The Waddell trial was set for Monday 15 November 1976. I was
not looking forward to it and felt that this expensive show-piece of a
trial would turn out to be a charade. It was not necessary, in the
public interest, to try and replace Meehan in Peterhead with Waddell.
I made no request, nor did my committee, for this. I feared a
catastrophic humiliation of Meehan, and was not let down. The trial
was to take place in Edinburgh High Court, where Meehan himself
had been convicted earlier. Ludovic Kennedy, Patrick Meehan, Michael
MacDonald and I were cited as Crown witnesses.

Glasgow's Queen Street Station, despite some modernisation, is a cold, cheerless, Victorian edifice, particularly so in the month of November. A fairly reliable half-hour service operates from Scotland's industrial capital in the west to the nominal capital in the east. Throughout the lengthy trial of Ian Waddell, regular commuters on the eight-thirty morning train must have been aware of the small, smart, dapper figure, who, daily, could be seen hurrying along Platform Two, clutching a pile of newspapers, and usually managing to cope with several cups of British Rail tea into the bargain. By his side, a petite, always anxious-looking figure. These were Paddy Meehan and his ever-faithful Betty.

Daily, they made the monotonous journey to and from the scene of his conviction. My wife, Delia, made the daily trip with them, as she followed the trial with almost as much interest as Meehan. She, too, had lived with the Meehan saga throughout these seven years.

As a witness I could not enter the court until I was called. At this trial, however, Lord Robertson did not want to hear what I had to say. Three times I entered the witness box to give evidence and twice I had to leave while the counsel debated whether what I could tell them was admissible. On the third occasion I was stopped altogether from giving evidence and made a reluctant departure from the Court. I felt frustrated and annoyed. At this stage the Crown abandoned its case against Dick and he was discharged from the dock.

When Meehan was called and mounted the three steps to the witness box to take the oath, his broad, pugnacious face showed none of the humour it had displayed on his journeys back and forwards to Edinburgh. Unbelievably, he was standing there not as a man whose conviction for murder had been quashed, but as a man impeached for the same crime.

Impatiently, he re-told his story of the actual events of that fateful night—and was treated with derision by both counsel for Waddell and by Lord Robertson.

But then Meehan did what many of us advised him not to do. He told a court, so scornful of his account of things, of other events which had preceded his own trial: of his certainty that the Special Branch was involved in his arrest and subsequent conviction for murder. (Mind you, with the more recent reading of books like *Spycatcher*, I now begin to wonder if there wasn't something in what Meehan claimed.)

If his previous evidence was derided by the Court, the Jury was left in no doubt as to how his theory was accepted by the Defence and

Lord Robertson. It must have been 'manna from heaven' so far as Mr Law Q.C., for Waddell, was concerned.

Defence counsel then went over the evidence Meehan had given at his own trial. His past criminal record was very properly referred to, frequently, and he was presented to the Jury as a man with neither scruples nor moral judgment. It was little wonder that, on numerous occasions, he lost his temper and shouted at his attackers, for such they were.

At one point, Lord Robertson asked in the somewhat unfriendly manner he used to address my client, 'Mr Meehan, even on your own submission, you must have passed through Ayr near the Ross house?'

'The car was not a time-machine,' Meehan snapped back. 'It could not leave Ayr in daylight and arrive in Kilmarnock in the dark.'

He was even asked if he had stayed in solitary confinement to avoid contact with other prisoners. It was suggested to him that he had bribed Ian Waddell to take the blame, and that he had approached other prisoners, confessing to the Ayr murder, and asking them to request Waddell to allow himself to be impeached—all of which he scornfully denied.

Time and again he tried to tell the Court of the identity parade where Abraham Ross was the last person, and not the first, to view the parade. As no evidence was to be led on this point, it was of no avail. I never thought the point mattered much anyway—although it obsessed Meehan.

The following was yet another brush with the bench:

Lord Robertson—'How have you been living since your release?'

Meehan—'I have been living on compensation of £2,500 paid on account.'

'Do you expect to get a lot more?'

'I expect so.'

'Did you know when you were in prison that you would get a lot of money when you came out?'

'I would expect, having got a Free Pardon, I would get compensation. I was offered £6,000 by the Scottish *Daily Record* and refused it. I got £2,000 from them.'

'Why was that?'

'For my story.'

'Are you getting any other money . . . from TV?'

'Oh yes. Two cheques for about £1,000.'

'A pretty lucrative affair this of yours . . . .'

'I don't think it's lucrative, considering I spent seven years in jail for something I didn't do.'

Patrick Meehan left the witness box—like myself, an extremely unhappy and frustrated man.

In his long-awaited summing-up, Lord Robertson launched a tirade of criticism couched against our Scottish Secretary for his having recommended Meehan's pardon. (This must have been one of the very few occasions when the judiciary publicly clashed with the Executive.) 'It was an action,' Lord Robertson thundered, 'which runs counter to the whole basis of justice and law in Scotland, [perhaps Lord Robertson had not been appraised of the Swanson pardon of the previous year] which is trial by Jury and the proper process of law [by this he may have meant 'impartial']. Such Executive interference meant that one of the greatest bulwarks of liberty in this country is threatened.'

The judge also gave his view on the meaning of 'pardon', saying, 'If you pardon someone, you pardoned him for something he had done, and not for something he had *not* done.' He went on to express concern at the advance publicity about matters bearing on the circumstances around the crimes with which Waddell was now charged, and the seven year delay in so doing.

He went on—'It is the very essence of the administration of justice in Scotland that an accused person comes into court without any previous publicity or speculation on the crime and his responsibility for it. It is an interesting speculation—what would have been the reaction of the jury at the Meehan trial, if his life-long record of crime and his proud claim to be an expert on safe-blowing, had been before them?'

With these latter comments, I am in entire agreement, and felt that the trial judge was right to highlight the dangers of prejudice to the accused by dint of prior publicity [although a measure of this was brought about by Waddell's own actions].

He went on, 'Waddell has very properly and understandably put in a special defence of impeachment against Meehan and Griffiths, alleging that the murder was committed by them. Not only has the Crown repeatedly implied that Meehan did not commit the crime, the media have given extensive publicity relating to him, in such terms as "The man wrongly convicted of murder".'

I agree, of course, with the trial judge, and it may be that he felt that he required to make a strong stand in this case, in order to eradicate any possibility of unfair prejudice towards the pannel, Ian Waddell.

As I have said, there is much justification for some of the hard-hitting points made by the trial judge. Waddell as an accused person was entitled to protection from such prejudice, and it was the duty of the presiding judge to ensure that this was, in fact, the case. There can be no doubt but that Lord Robertson amply discharged this important and difficult duty—but where can one draw the line in this situation? Can he be faulted for perhaps going too far to achieve the requisite standard of fairness at Waddell's trial? I think not. This might account for his making it patently obvious that, in his view, as he said, Meehan still appeared to be guilty along with Griffiths, all to the exclusion of the man on trial—Waddell.

The judge's task was an extremely difficult and unusual one and, in fairness to him, he showed remarkable strength and conviction. It is regrettable, however, that Meehan was made to bear the brunt of this although at least he was out of prison ... whereas there was always the possibility for Waddell to spend many years of his life there, but for the judge's strong and determined approach. Lord Robertson was quite correct in saying that we cannot have trial by media.

The jury retired for a period of one hour and ten minutes, and returned with an acquittal verdict by majority.

As Waddell was led from the dock with Jury discharged, and now free to serve the remainder of his 18-months' sentence for violence, Mrs Betty Meehan stood up in the public benches and screamed hysterically at him, 'You are guilty, you are guilty.'

Waddell, in his turn, shouted, 'Now you know the truth. No, I am not guilty, your man's guilty.'

Court ushers then rushed towards Mrs Meehan—Patrick Meehan had left the Court in high dudgeon at a much earlier stage—and, almost in tears, she cried, 'Seven years and four months he waited for this.' Mrs Meehan was then taken from the packed courtroom and Lord Robertson left the bench, for the last time in this most memorable case.

Meanwhile, on the day of Meehan's pardon and release, Fairbairn, on my instructions, had asked the Scottish Secretary, Bruce Millan, in Parliament, for a public enquiry into the whole matter of Meehan's case.

22

Following the scathing attacks by Lord Robertson at Waddell's trial—attacks on both the Government and the Lord Advocate—it was finally announced in March 1977, by Millan, that there would be an independent inquiry set up to look into the Meehan affair (this must also include compensation—we had refused Bruce Weir's earlier pittance). No doubt Millan was still smarting from the powerful attack made by Robertson in his memorable charge to the jury, only a few months earlier.

Immunity from prosecution was to be given to all witnesses at this inquiry. Both Meehan and I were anxious to have a Public Inquiry, but neither of us were 'over the moon' about the immunity clause. This inquiry, however, had been ordered by Parliament and would be held in private, being undertaken by Lord Hunter, Senator of the College of Justice in Scotland. It was further stated that the findings would be made public, and published in due course.

His terms of reference were, 'To carry out an independent examination of the available information relating to the murder of Mrs Rachel Ross, at Ayr in July, 1969, and the action taken by the police, the Crown Office and the Scottish Home and Health Department.'

But the terms of reference would not extend to the making of any judgment about the guilt or innocence of Meehan or Waddell, or the reasons for and justification of Meehan's Royal Pardon.

The long-awaited inquiry was announced by Millan in Parliament, in answer to a question by James White, Labour MP for Partick. Millan pointed out that there had already been two trials for the murder of Mrs Ross, with Meehan obtaining a pardon and Waddell being acquitted:

> It would be wrong in principle, in my view and potentially unfair to Meehan and Waddell, for an inquiry to call in question such past issues. It is also an important principle that the Secretary of State, having regard to the nature of the decisions taken, cannot be obliged to give detailed reasons in justification of his decisions in individual cases, whether or not to make a recommendation for the exercise of the Royal Prerogative of Mercy.

Lord Hunter was a man of exceptionally high intellect, sharp and strong in every way. I welcomed his appointment, and, as I saw it, his impartiality. Ludovic Kennedy would have been happier had the Chairman been selected from the English Bar, someone like Louis Blom-Cooper QC. Someone who had not been affected by the network of the whole Ayr case. I remember meeting Ludo and trying to allay any fears that he had on the subject of the Chairman of this inquiry. But I did not have the benefit of hindsight!

Meehan was afraid that the private inquiry would turn into another official 'whitewash'. Knowing Hunter, as I thought I did, I told Meehan that he was painstaking and fair in his approach. Short of going to England—heaven forbid!—I considered Hunter to be the ideal choice. In addition, he had had no prior dealings with the Meehan affair. At first, however, I felt it would be pointless to meet Lord Hunter, because of the narrow terms of his remit—but, following a personal request from Lord Hunter, I agreed.

Meehan had agreed with me at first—but he also changed his mind on my advice.

Before doing so, he said: 'I will not take part in the inquiry, because it is to be in private. I would rather go back to prison than appear before an inquiry behind closed doors. If it is secret, then I want nothing to do with it. I want a public investigation.' He was perhaps being a bit melodramatic, I thought.

In all, I had three lengthy meetings with Hunter in Glasgow. These were informal, in that we were casually dressed and, apart from a shorthand writer, only his secretary, a Mr Keegan, was present.

At the first meeting, in June 1977, I appeared with my mother-in-law, Mrs Fallon (now deceased), who was extremely nervous. Lord Hunter allowed me to be present with her when she spoke of the conversation she had had with Griffiths on the day of Meehan's arrest. She spoke of his English accent, and was then thoroughly cross-examined by him in that regard. I began to wonder.

My sessions with him were much lengthier, and I was impressed by the homework he had done on the case. He knew *almost* as much as I did about the case—but not quite. His questions were extremely pertinent and searching. I started, correctly I thought, on the premise that Meehan was innocent. I made the point several times but gathered that Hunter was little impressed.

He produced many of Meehan's pre-trial defence sheets—a mountain of notes—so voluminous that I had not the time, nor the inclination, to read and digest all of them. Going over these I was amazed at how accurate some of the points had been. There were hundreds of lines of inquiry suggested, but, regrettably, one had only 24 hours in a day—and one required to eat and sleep as well.

After each session, I felt tired and drained of energy. Our second session started at 2 p.m. and finished at 7 p.m. I had to rush from there to the Sherbrooke Hotel in Pollokshields, where I had agreed to speak at a local Catenian Circle Meeting on a well-known criminal case—you will guess the title.

I left the Sherbrooke at midnight, and stumbled into my bed at 12.45 a.m. On occasions like this—and there were many—I would ask myself if the whole 'shooting match' had been worth it. But the answer had to be, 'Yes, definitely.'

By Christmas Day 1980, I began to wonder what had happened to the Hunter Report.

But the report was published, eventually—over five years after my first interview with Hunter—in August 1982, when I was on holiday in the land of my ancestors, Switzerland. For two days I received telephone calls from the Press of Britain and Europe. Even the *Sunday Times* carried front page cover of my brush with Hunter on the matter of confidentiality and the stand taken by me. As we will see, he criticised me on not a few occasions.

The proprietrix of the 'Beau Rivage' in Weggis, near Lucerne, must have been impressed. As I say, for two whole days there were constant calls from all over. Before we left, she sent three bottles of Krug Champagne to our bedroom, with the compliments of the house. She then became particularly interested in my returning there next year. But three bottles of the best champagne did not persuade me to holiday there again—nor would I, the weather having been dreadful.

The Hunter Report, in my view, was extremely disappointing, particularly as the cost to the ratepayer was a mammoth £330,826. It took five years to produce and turned out to be somewhat turgid, convoluted and dull.

Hunter severely criticised myself, on many counts. Perhaps we can do unwise things while enveloped in a feeling of total unfairness, and the fragmentation of our inherent hopes that the system of justice simply cannot miscarry.

At one meeting, he suggested that I should have gone to the police at once, following 'Tank's' first confession to me. This shows a total inability to assess a real situation from the lofty perch of an ivory tower.

He went on to say that any conversations I had with McGuinness were *not* confidential for some obscure reason. He added that I should have gone to the police after my interview with Skiverton, too.

My answer was that Lord Hunter had never been a solicitor and should listen to the experience of one with many years behind him who said, without fear of contradiction, that intimate conversations between solicitor and client are confidential in the extreme. I back my experience against that of Hunter—in this aspect—any day of the week.

In volume three (page 1233) Hunter introduces a four-man-theory embracing the possibility of Griffiths, Meehan, Waddell, and McGuinness all being involved in the crime. So much for his terms of reference, which I thought were too narrow. It was speculation such as this which, I think, caused Meehan to be convicted in the first place.

Hunter seemed—indeed, was—hostile both to Meehan and myself. He suggested that the defence should have challenged the police about the paper found on Griffiths. I remonstrated that Griffiths was dead, and that we had no specific instructions to do this.

So often, in the early, dark years of Meehan, the factor of the jury's verdict was thrown in my face. Repeatedly, in correspondence with the Lord Advocate and the Scottish Secretary, it was stated that, 'The jury in its wisdom saw fit to convict and we cannot, and will not, go behind their findings.'

This attitude seemed to pre-empt proper independent consideration of our many cogent and salient points. True, very often juries arrive at the correct conclusion (perhaps not always for the right reasons), but to take a stand to the effect that this is necessarily exhaustive and foolproof cannot surely apply when dealing, as we are, with mere mortals.

I recall from the very early days, after conviction, that I suggested to the Crown authorities that in my view Meehan was innocent, as was Griffiths, and I asked them to send one of their officials to the prison to interview Meehan, and to assess him—his asides, his answers and his entire demeanour. Had this unusual course of action been acted upon, so much time and expense might well have been saved.

I pointed out that I had, after all, represented even then more persons charged with murder than anyone else (alive or dead). I was not in the habit of protesting over a guilty verdict, unless there was proper cause. One would have thought that my vehement protestations following this verdict would have caused someone in authority to pause and discuss the matter in depth, either with me or with someone else, instead of merely quoting the majority verdict of the jury, which was, after all, only too well known to me.

Yes, Meehan will be remembered long after they have all passed on, as, one hopes, will be the various lessons to be learnt from the whole saga. A situation like this must, I pray, never be allowed to recur. Before the Hunter Report eventually surfaced in late 1982, two of the battle-scarred protagonists had been slain by the sword—Winning, in 1980, and Waddell, in 1982. There are few of us left, and I begin to feel just a little privileged!

John 'Gypsy' Winning was killed in February 1980 in a house at Rosebank Cottage, Dunfermline. I was instructed by the powerful James McLellan, who was charged with murdering him by punching and kicking him repeatedly about the head and body, knocking him to the ground, stamping repeatedly on his head and striking him with a kettle. The trial was fixed for Perth High Court, on 16 June 1980.

It emerged clearly that Winning had been quite drunk and had picked a fight with my client, McLellan—somewhat unwisely, as events established. The fracas, in the main, had been started and dominated by Winning, who met my other client, McLellan, for the first time at the cottage, and grossly underestimated him. McLellan's father had been a well-known street fighter and the son had picked up a lot on his way. The Crown accepted from us a plea to culpable homicide on the grounds of undoubted provocation and McLellan was sentenced to a period of 30 months' imprisonment, backdated to the day of his arrest.

Ian Waddell was murdered in mid-1982, in a house at Blackthorn Street, Glasgow, by a friend of his, Andy Gentle, now serving life imprisonment. He (Waddell) had been concerned in the murder of a Mrs Josephine Chipperfield, along with Gentle, and had met his end by strangulation when Gentle had formed the view that there was more than a possibility that Waddell might inform on him to the police.

No one would argue, surely, that he was any great loss to society at large. After the jury's verdict, Gentle's counsel had only this to say, 'Despite his name, he is not.' The same, in fact, could be said of his victim.

As I now enter the closing stages of this mammoth case I feel just a little disappointed. I have enjoyed so much the writing of this saga and realise that I shall never have as momentous an epic as this again.

As I said earlier, Meehan asked me officially in 1982 to act for him in respect of his damages claim. He made it clear that he would take the matter to the civil courts if necessary, in a series of actions. The reader should note that at this late stage of the proceedings the instructions were coming from Meehan himself, not the police. I agreed to act and ascertained that he had not been requested to hand back the sum of £2,500 paid to account, in advance of the previous offer. I told him that we would require to wait for the Hunter Report, which, I thought would be imminent.

He agreed and I assured him that whereas any damages claim was not in Hunter's remit, there could be no settlement until this Hunter Report was published.

I saw little of Meehan between 1977 and 1982—just the odd telephone call, looking for reassurance, and the occasional visit.

Waiting five years for the Hunter Report proved to be frustrating for both of us. He would come to the office and ask me when the Report would surface and if it would be favourable. I would remind him that, regrettably, I did not have a crystal ball. I would tell him that the unbelievably lengthy time for the Report must mean absolute thoroughness on the part of Hunter.

I knew that, following the Report, we would go back to Parliament, yet once more, through Fairbairn, and request a re-appraisal of Meehan's claim for compensation. I agreed to write to the Scottish Secretary at this time, and point out, forcibly, that the procedure adopted by James Law QC in the Swanson compensation should be followed. Law had been very thorough, and saw relevant witnesses and heard my submissions. The powers-that-be must surely follow this precedent, which would give them an excuse to withdraw Bruce Weir's wholly inadequate assessment.

Both of us had no option but to wait for Hunter, not thinking that it would be a five-year sojourn. I dearly hoped that, at last, the authorities would wish to draw a double line under the Meehan file, confine it to a secure box in the archives, and settle by offering an acceptable figure. After all, it was time everyone called it a day.

The Hunter Report in August 1982 caused a slight setback and embryonic distress signals fluttered fleetingly for the ensuing eleven months. Meehan told me that he should not have accepted my advice to appear before Hunter. I disagreed, stating that his non-co-operation would have dampened his prospects of compensation. Yes, there was friction between us, once more. Despite our brushes, I continued, inexorably, to pursue the Scottish Secretary with request upon request for the re-assessment of his due compensation.

On 15 July 1983 the Secretary of State for Scotland announced in the Commons that David A. O. Edward QC, had accepted his invitation to make a fresh assessment of the amount of compensation to be offered to Meehan. The terms of the remit were:

> You are invited to tender advice to the Secretary of State, on what sum of money, as at the date of your report, should be paid by way of compensation to Meehan. You are not required to make detailed findings of fact, but simply to narrate the matters which you have taken into account.
>
> You must then recommend an amount for compensation. You should not entertain representations from any person other than the Secretary of State or the claimant (Meehan) or his solicitor, Mr Beltrami.

I had considerable correspondence with Mr Edward on the matter of damages, in the main what we lawyers call *solatium*, that is, damages for the injured feelings of being locked-up, wrongly and for all of seven years. Pecuniary loss also required to be considered, such as loss of earnings over this period (not a rock-solid ground, as his work record was not of the best), loss of future earning capacity and additional matters, such as expenses incurred by the family in their frequent visits to Peterhead.

It is interesting to note this in the remit—'for whatever relevance it may have, the fact that, when you were convicted of the murder, you were also convicted of other offences (theft and passport offences) and that, on your own admission, you were planning another crime at the time of the murder. . .'. Meehan had not been sentenced for these other matters as the Crown had not moved for sentence—moving only in respect of the murder conviction. In that event, the sentence of life imprisonment was mandatory.

I forwarded to Mr Edward notes on inflation since 1969, a survey on this done by the *Evening Times* newspaper's financial expert, details of the Swanson compensation paid in 1975 and details of several English cases involving wrongful imprisonment. I also underlined the dreadful type of murder that he had been convicted of—an elderly and decent lady.

I compared Swanson's award of £5,000 in 1975 for a mere bank robbery (he served 11 months of a five-year sentence) with the fact that Meehan had been branded a vicious, nasty killer of an old, defenceless woman in her own home.

In our private meetings, Meehan told me that he formed the view that he should receive the sum of £100,000 but I did not think that this would be possible.

The letter-writing finished, a meeting was arranged by Edward, for 26 September 1983, at his Heriot Row home in Edinburgh. Time was set for 10 a.m.

Meehan and I were afraid that the unfriendly terms of the Hunter Report might undermine our prospects. Accordingly, I decided on a bold, possibly disastrous, course of action. Inevitably, I had to take Meehan along with me on this tactical manoeuvre.

When I arrived outside Edward's home, the place was awash with Pressmen and TV camera crews. I was asked about the prospects, but hedged the answers.

Meehan was already inside. I fought my way through the Press ranks and rang the bell. An embarrassed David Edward ushered me in, where I saw Meehan in the study seated at a desk.

I stood at the seat next to Meehan and said to Edward, who was about to sit down, 'Before we start, if you intend to pay any attention whatsoever to the Hunter Report, then we are off. There would be no point wasting your time and ours.'

He was clearly taken aback and caught off-guard—which was our intention. He asked me to wait, as he would require to make several telephone calls on that point. He left two anxious men in his study, returning after 20 minutes. He said, simply, 'I shall pay no attention to the Report.'

I retorted, 'A good thing, too—let's proceed.'

The meeting lasted until 1 p.m., when both Meehan and I left.

The Press, patient as they are, were still outside *en masse*. I expressed my satisfaction and said, 'I am confident that the 15-year saga is now nearing its end.'

Months elapsed—and a lot of speculation. As I waited, I had a feeling lurking in the back of my mind: what if he nominates a derisory sum, as Bruce Weir had done? Where would we go from there? Apart from spending so much time with Meehan, I wanted, desperately, to terminate matters for good. The prospect of a continuing fight was not a pleasant one. I prayed for victory and final success and consoled myself by thinking that Edward and the Government also wanted to rid themselves of this embarrassing and costly case.

The abortive Waddell trial would have cost the taxpayer upwards of £250,000 and the Hunter Report, as I have already said, cost almost £350,000.

I wrote to Edward suggesting that Meehan and I should be the first persons to know of his findings. He agreed. I did not want public debates on the propriety or otherwise of his assessment. It was arranged that I would be briefed exactly one hour before the media.

In February 1984 it came—an award of £50,500. Admittedly, I had argued for a figure of £100,000 but, in the back of my mind, I was quite happy to settle for the figure nominated by Edward.

At the hearing in Heriot Row, there had been one item of claim which I have not mentioned so far. This was a heading 'Legal Expenses'. When this matter was raised, I advised Edward that I did not wish to make any claim whatsoever by way of legal costs. I suggested that everything should go to Meehan who was the aggrieved person. I had acted on a compelling matter of principle—there was no pecuniary enticement.

The *One O'clock News* had Meehan rejecting the offer out of hand. I contacted him within the hour and convinced him to accept the offer, as also did his wife. I honestly think he wanted to accept in any event, but preferred, publicly, to be seen to be pushed.

Within days, I handed over his St Andrew's House cheque, but Meehan, as always phlegmatic, did not seem to enthuse. He may have thanked me—I wouldn't be certain—but he disappeared out of the office and, incidentally, out of my life.

I must confess that I had never been a fan of Meehan's—but what did that matter?—the principle is often greater and more attractive than the individual. In his favour, it must be said that he, like Swanson, has never offended since the Queen saw fit to single him out as a person justifiably aggrieved.

APPENDIX I

Extract from Parliament's *Hansard*:
Patrick Meehan

Secretary of State for Scotland (Bruce Millan):

As the House knows, I have been considering the case of Patrick Meehan. Patrick Meehan was charged with the murder of Mrs Abraham Ross at Ayr, and on 24th October 1969, in the High Court of Justiciary in Edinburgh, was convicted of the murder and sentenced to Life Imprisonment.

He appealed against his conviction to the Court of Criminal Appeal, and, after a hearing, his appeal was dismissed on 25th November, 1969.

Since that time there have been representations regarding the conviction to successive Secretaries of State for Scotland based on the case against Mr Meehan at the trial, but also on other matters, including statements by another man alleging his participation in the robbery and murder.

In the last few days I have received new information following the death of William McGuinness, a man with a record of crimes of dishonesty and violence. It was revealed after his death that he had made statements to the effect that he had participated in the Ross robbery to the exclusion of Mr Meehan.

The value of these statements must remain a matter of judgment, but there is independent evidence establishing that Mr McGuinness was in Ayr on the night of the murder. I have considered whether the case might again be brought under judicial review.

The only provision of law by which a conviction, once reached and appealed against, can be restored to the judicial field is my power to refer a case back under section 63 (1A) of the Criminal Procedure (Scotland) Act, 1975. However, by statute, the Court could not go wider in considering the case than it can in an ordinary appeal against conviction, and, having regard to the nature of the considerations relevant to a decision of the case, I have reached the conclusion that my powers of reference back are inappropriate to it.

Nor would further investigation or enquiry be likely to lead to the discovery of such further information as to make such a reference appropriate.

In the circumstances I have reached a conclusion that it falls to me as Secretary of State to reach a decision of whether or not to recommend the exercise of the Royal Prerogative on the new information which has become available since the death of McGuinness.

I have therefore decided to recommend the exercise of the Royal Prerogative to grant a Free Pardon. Mr Meehan is being released today.

My Right Honourable and learned friend the Lord Advocate is at present considering, in light of the new evidence, whether he should instruct any further investigations with a view to possible criminal proceedings.

Mr Buchanan Smith: 'May I say how much I appreciate that the decision of the Right Honourable Gentleman, the one that he has announced, cannot have been an easy one and must have involved him in a great deal of thought and consideration. Will he confirm that the new evidence that he now describes in his statement, which was not available when this case was considered on previous occasions, is available now only because a Solicitor concerned (Mr Beltrami) is no longer bound by the Confidentiality Rule?

'Does this not raise very much wider questions and might it not be appropriate that the matter of solicitor's confidentiality should be referred to the Royal Commission on the legal profession? Secondly, would the Right Honourable Gentleman say whether the police had been involved in the recent investigation and confirm that they have co-operated fully in bringing this new evidence to light?'

Mr Millan: 'I can confirm that the new information, which I received only recently, is important and has weighed very heavily in the decision I have taken. Solicitor's confidentiality raises many extremely difficult questions and is, I think, in the first instance, a matter for the Law Society of Scotland. As far as I'm aware, it would be relevant for the Royal Commission to consider that matter, but, if there were thought to be some benefit to be gained from any discussions between my officials and the Law Society, I would be happy to co-operate on that.

'I can confirm, on the second point, that we have had the utmost police co-operation in these further investigations.'

Mr Robert Hughes: 'Can I press my Right Honourable friend further on the question of confidentiality? Since this question was first raised, there is now a clear example of a Miscarriage of Justice.

'Although I welcome the decision which my Right Honourable friend has taken, is it not the case that previous Secretaries of State have been severely handicapped by lack of knowledge which was available in another quarter?'

Mr Millan: 'That may be so. I have said already that I have had additional information available to me which was not available to my predecessors. I have absolutely no doubt that my predecessors considered this case with great care and anxiety. However, on the question of confidentiality of information given to solicitors, an obvious point, for example, is whether the information would be made available to solicitors if there were no Confidentiality Rule. It is not a matter which is easy to decide.'

Mr Fairbairn: 'Does the House appreciate that this is a moment of great triumph for those who have been fighting for Meehan's release for seven years against the bland face of the Scottish Office and the Lord Advocate?'

Mr Robert Hughes: 'That is disgraceful!'

Mr Fairbairn: 'In a moment of victory magnanimity is essential, but does the Secretary of State appreciate that this case raises a large number of important questions which can be answered only by a Public Enquiry as to why, for instance, evidence of paper from the safe of Mr Ross was found in the pockets of a man who is now acknowledged to be innocent, or of his accomplice, who is now acknowledged to be innocent, and how the parade was arranged? Many other questions must now be answered as to how, again and again, both the Courts and the Secretaries of State have frustrated Honorary Members too long.'

Mr Mellish: 'On a point of order, Mr Speaker, I have no interest in the matter, but as a member of this House I always thought that the Chair had strictly ruled on allegations of imputations being made here against individuals who are unable to defend themselves in a case of this kind. Other Honorary Members have never been allowed to go this far. I ask you, is this not the case where you ought to stop it?'

Mr Speaker: 'I am much obliged to the Right Honourable Gentlemen, but I have not yet heard an allegation against an individual.'

Mr Fairbairn: 'Does the House appreciate that we must have an explanation of how the Lord Advocate and those succeeding him took the right of their office to oppose Bills of Criminal Letters which would have established the very facts which are now admitted in the House by the Secretary of State?'

Mr Millan: 'I do not think I can accept that point. The fact is, there was a conviction and an appeal, and the appeal was turned down. Many other matters raised subsequently were matters considered at the trial, as the Honourable and learned Gentleman, Mr Fairbairn, should know, since he was the defending Counsel. All I can say on this matter, which is a very difficult one, is that it is a very responsible decision, indeed, to set aside a conviction in one of the High Courts in this land. Any Secretary of State would have to be very well-persuaded of what he was doing before he would set aside a conviction and take the decision I have taken today.

'As far as the question of an independent enquiry is concerned, if the Honourable and learned Gentleman will look at the statement I have made, he will see that I have finished by saying that my Right Honourable and learned friend, the Lord Advocate, was making some further enquiries into certain aspects of this case. I would be, at the very least, premature to consider any question of an independent enquiry before these investigations had been completed.'

Mr William Ross: 'While not necessarily disagreeing with the final decision which my Right Honourable friend reached, may I ask whether he appreciates that in this case there has been a confusion and a duplication of confessions, not all from unimpeachable sources, which makes this matter much more difficult? Bearing in mind the important implicit consequences of his decision for many people in Scotland, is he satisfied that this was the only action which was open to him?

'Will he publish the police report about which we have read, which he received, and will he make it clear that the original defending solicitor, Mr Beltrami, had in his possession a confession not from the man who was accused in the defence by the Honourable and learned Member for Kinross and West Perthshire (Mr Fairbairn)—that was his Special Defence, accusing somebody else—but a third man, whose confession is now being accepted?'

Mr Millan: 'So far as Waddell is concerned, that was a matter raised during the trial. I agree very much with my Right Honourable friend that this is a case of very considerable complexity. All these matters must be extremely difficult, and this, for a whole host of reasons, is a particularly difficult one. I know that my Right Honourable friend applied the very high standards of care and diligence to his consideration of this case that he applied to all other matters with which he dealt at the Scottish Office.

'I have come to a different conclusion from my Right Honourable friend, but I have had certain additional information available to me which was not available to him when he was Secretary of State for Scotland.

'As I have said, that additional information has weighed very heavily with me. My Right Honourable friend asks whether the decision I have reached is the only decision I could have reached. Of course, it is not the only decision—I could have taken other decisions, but it was the only decision I felt I could reasonably reach, in the light of all the information available to me.

'So far as the publication of the police reports is concerned, these are, in the nature of things, confidential documents. It would be very undesirable to breach the principle that these reports—which, of course, go not to me but to the Crown Agent and the Lord Advocate—should be published after the event even if, in particular circumstances, there is a lot of public interest and people may well feel that certain interests of justice would be served by publication.

'I do not think that I can take the view that these police reports should be published. But, as I have said, my Right Honourable and learned friend the Lord Advocate is carrying out further investigations and it is certainly my intention that we should investigate the matter with very great vigour and thoroughness.'

Mr Buchan: 'I, too, congratulate the Secretary of State on taking the decision. I have called for an enquiry but I believe that the course that he has chosen to be correct and just in the prevailing situation. Although he must, as I do, reject the allegations of the Honourable and learned Member for Kinross and West Perthshire, Mr Fairbairn, which amounted to almost prejudging the very enquiry we seek, will the points mentioned in relation to the evidence be matters which will be under enquiry both in relation to a possible criminal prosecution and in a wider context?'

Mr Millan: 'With the possibility of criminal proceedings being involved, the matters which may be the subject of enquiry are specific matters for my Right Honourable and learned friend the Lord Advocate, and not for me. However, I can say that all aspects of these matters, including some which immediately come to mind, will certainly be investigated, so far as they can be investigated at this date. I know that my Right

Honourable and learned friend will not mind my saying that he certainly intends to see that all relevant matters are thoroughly investigated.'

Mrs Winifred Ewing: 'May I, on behalf of the Glasgow Bar Association, of which I am a former President, congratulate the Secretary of State on what cannot have been an easy decision to make?'

Mr English: 'May I reinforce my Right Honourable friend's gentle suggestion that the Honourable Member for North Angus (Mr Buchanan-Smith) is wrong about confidentiality? What sane man would be likely to confess to a murder save to a person who is not allowed to give that confession as evidence in Court? It is very important to preserve confidentiality between lawyer and client—which, in this case, has caused a man to be released.'

Mr Millan: 'I do not think that I want to comment any more on this, but I think that the solicitor himself may take the view that, if it had not been for the convention of confidentiality, it is doubtful whether the information given to him would, in fact, have been given to him.'

Mr Younger: 'As there was intense public interest in this case, would the Right Honourable Gentleman please take the greatest care to ensure that the maximum fairness and impartiality is achieved, particularly with reference to the conduct of the police in this case? Since they do a very difficult and dangerous task in many ways for the benefit of the public, will the Right Honourable Gentleman ensure that they are not the subject of a witch-hunt in this case?'

Mr Millan: 'I have paid tribute a number of times to the Scottish Police Force and I am happy to do so again. At the same time, as far as any of these matters involve policemen, they will be investigated with the same rigour and thoroughness as if they involved ordinary citizens.'

Mr Hughes: 'On a point of order, Mr Speaker, one appreciates the deep concern of the Honourable and learned Member of Kinross and West Perthshire (Mr Fairbairn) on this matter, and the great fight that he has waged for years for his client, but has it not always been a convention of the House that an Advocate does not personally raise or discuss in this House any matter which concerns a case in which he has been directly involved? I appreciate that you allowed the question, and that the Honourable and learned Member has raised it previously, but it does set a dangerous precedent on other completely different cases. Should not this matter be considered a little more by yourself and the appropriate committee to see if a Rule could not be introduced?'

Mr Speaker: 'I'm obliged to the Honourable and learned Member. As the House has seen, I have just had the "good book" given to me. It says, "It is contrary to the usage and derogatory to the dignity of this House that any of its members should bring forward, promote or advocate in this House any proceeding or measure in which he may have acted or been concerned for, or in consideration of, a pecuniary fee or reward." I will obviously look at the matter.'

So ends the relevant *Hansard* passage, dated 19 May 1976—the day of Meehan's release from Peterhead Prison.

APPENDIX II

As a consequence of the Meehan identification parade at Turnbull Street in 1969, and the surprise with which the possibility of identification by 'voice' emerged, the procedure has been altered. The present situation, and a much more satisfactory one, is that each witness—before looking at the line-up—is given the following instruction:

> You will now be shown the parade. You should look at the line-up, studying each one. You may ask for all or any of them to turn around, to stand side-on, to walk, to talk, to speak, to do all or any of these, or to do anything you wish. Simply tell me if you have any requests and I will do my best to meet them. You can make such requests at any time. Have you any requests?

At this stage the solicitor would know if the parade were to be the normal type (like 90 per cent) or something 'special', such as voice identification.

This occurs before the witness views, and so there is no reason why the solicitor should now be caught 'on the hop'.

I do not blame the police for this occurrence at Meehan's parade. There were no rules in writing at that stage. Now the whole matter of parades has been formalised for the benefit of everyone.

GLOSSARY OF LEGAL TERMS

Adjournment Debate: Consists of a 15-minute point raised at the end of a Parliamentary day (very often after midnight) by a Backbencher. Notice must be given of the subject and a Minister is obliged to reply.

Adminicle: Any piece of supporting evidence.

Advocate: The equivalent of the English Barrister. All advocates are members of the Faculty of Advocates and are governed by a Dean. Their main duties are to plead in the Court of Session and High Court of Justiciary and have sole right of audience there. This state of affairs might well be altered in the foreseeable future as a result of Government activity. After a number of years (at least 12) an Advocate may be invited to take silk as in England and become a Queen's Counsel (QC). He is then known as senior counsel and, until recently, only appeared in Court when assisted by a junior counsel. Qualifications for Advocates and Solicitors are identical. Advocates also give opinions on unusual points of law.

Concert: In normal circumstances each person is responsible for his own criminal acts. However if two or more persons take part in a criminal plot or plan or, in other words, a joint criminal enterprise (acting in concert), then each one is responsible for the actions of the others. Take for example a bank robbery where *A* sits in the driver's seat of the getaway car, *B* stands at the corner and acts as look-out and *C* enters the bank and robs the teller—all are jointly responsible for the robbery. *A* and *B* were not even in the bank but played a part in the common plan. There can be accession before the fact (planning, etc), accession at the time of the crime but not, apart from treason, *after* the fact in Scotland. Different principles apply in England.

Conspiracy: Is when two or more persons agree to render one another assistance in doing an act—whether as an end or as means to an end—

which would be criminal if done by a single individual. Such is an extension to the law of criminal attempts and is completed by *agreement* to commit substantive crime. The prosecution of such a crime has become more common in recent years in Scotland, although it has always been regularly used in England.

Culpable Homicide: Is killing arising from an unlawful act or omission where death would not be foreseen as a probable consequence i.e., a killing caused by such an unlawful act but lacking in the deliberate intention to kill which would have made the charge one of murder (see below). The English form is *manslaughter*. There are three kinds:

(1) Killing in circumstances implying murder but for diminished responsibility in the accused.

(2) Homicide by doing an unlawful act, where death would not reasonably be foreseen as the probable consequence of the act.

(3) Homicide from negligence, or from rashness in the performance of lawful duty.

Declaration: Is a statement relevant to the charge made by the person accused on the occasion of his first appearance before the Sheriff. It is not made on oath and is recorded in long hand by the Sheriff and Clerk of Court. The accused is not cross-examined on it and, eventually, it may be lodged as a production in the case and referred to at the trial.

Domicile of Citation Sisted at the Sheriff Clerk's Office: When a person charged has been granted bail on solemn matters (i.e., Sheriff and Jury or High Court) his address (for the purpose of serving papers such as Indictment or Notices) is accepted as being the Sheriff Clerk's Office of the Court where he first appeared and was granted bail. Accordingly, there is a duty on the bailed person to check, periodically, with the Sheriff Clerk at his office. In fact, copies of all official documents are also served on his solicitor who would, or should, advise his client in any event.

Evidence: The testimony of eye-witnesses is direct evidence; indirect (circumstantial) evidence consists of circumstances, admitted or proved, from which the existence of a fact is inferred. Examples are fibres, paint scrapings, fingerprints, traces of blood, etc.

Hamesucken: Consists of a violent assault upon a person in his own dwelling, entry having been gained for that purpose. Formerly this was a capital crime.

High Court of Justiciary: The Supreme Criminal Court of Scotland, dealing with the more serious crimes which are prosecuted by the Lord Advocate and his Deputes. The judges are the Lord Justice General (who presides over the First Division of the Appeal Court), the Lord Justice Clerk (who chairs the Second) and the Lords Commissioners of Justiciary. All these are also judges of the Court of Session—the Supreme Civil Court of which the Lord Justice General is Lord President. These appointments are made by the Queen.

Indictment (Pronounced Inditement): After being served with the Indictment (the formal written accusation or charge made out in the name of the Lord

Advocate), the accused appeared—for the first time in public at a pleading diet before the Sheriff. At this diet he was required to plead Guilty or Not Guilty and any special defences (see below) applicable to the case were lodged by the defence. This diet was a minimum period of 10 days before the trial. In the event of a plea of Guilty, the accused would be sentenced on the spot or, if need be, remitted to the High Court. In the event of a plea of Not Guilty, the case was simply continued to the trial diet. At all High Court Pleading Diets the matter was simply continued to the Diet of Trial. However, since the Criminal Procedure (Scotland) Act, 1975 and the Criminal Justice (Scotland) Act, 1980, pleading diets were done away with. Since the abolition of the pleading diet the defence simply lodge any special defence at least 10 days before the trial. These documents are lodged in the hands of the Sheriff Clerk in Sheriff Court matters and in the hands of the Clerk of Justiciary in matters referring to the High Court. The writer did not agree with the abolition of the pleading diet in view of the fact that it was a convenient opportunity to discuss matters with the Prosecutor some time before the trial, as well as alerting one to its imminence.

Interdict (in England Injunction): A Civil Court order restricting the activities of individuals or corporate bodies on cause shown.

Law Society: The governing body of solicitors. This body has power to investigate the affairs of solicitors and, indeed, prosecute and punish in the event of negligence or serious omission by them. Difficult matters encountered in practice should be directed to this body which has a duty to instruct and guide its members. On the matter of the writer's position *vis à vis* confidentiality, the Society stalled, eventually refusing to face up to the unique situation. I have never been one of their favourite lads—nor will I ever be.

Lord Advocate: The prosecution of solemn or indictable crime in Scotland is in the hands of the Lord Advocate and of subordinate public prosecutors acting under his control. The Lord Advocate has the universal and exclusive title to prosecute on indictment. The Solicitor-General (his next in command) and the Advocate-Depute are his deputies. In extremely serious cases the prosecution is normally done by a Law Officer i.e., the Lord Advocate or the Solicitor-General. Both of these appointments are of a full-time nature whereas the appointment of Advocate Depute is part-time. The Lord Advocate selects his deputes. In solemn procedure in the Sheriff Court the public prosecutor is the Procurator Fiscal and he takes instructions from the Lord Advocate, the indictment being signed by the Fiscal upon the authority of the Lord Advocate. In High Court matters the indictment is normally signed by an Advocate Depute on behalf of the Lord Advocate. He is also the Minister of the Crown responsible to Parliament for matters relating to the administration of law in Scotland including the investigation and prosecution of all crime.

Murder: Is constituted by any wilful act causing the destruction of life, whether intended to kill, or displaying such wicked recklessness as to imply a disposition depraved enough to be regardless of consequences. No motive need be established.

Nobile Officium: The High Court will only exercise its *nobile officium* where the circumstances are extraordinary or unforeseen and where no other remedy or procedure is provided by the Law. This power can be invoked only by a *quorum* of the Court, and not by a single judge. It has been said that the *nobile officium* is invoked to interpose, to modify or abate the rigour of the Law and, to a certain extent, to give aid where no remedy could be had in a Court confined to strict law. The *nobile officium* or duty of this Court may, within limits, mitigate the strictness of the common law.

Not Proven: An intermediate verdict alternative to 'Guilty' or 'Not Guilty' available under our Scottish Criminal procedure to a Court or Jury, having the same effect as 'Not Guilty' but appropriate where there is suspicion of guilt with conclusive evidence lacking. Such a verdict is peculiar to Scotland and is often described as a 'halfway house' where innocence has not been established, nor has proof of guilt beyond reasonable doubt. A safeguard against miscarriage of justice. Put another way, 'If there is to be error then err on the side of safety and acquit by such a verdict'. In the event of a verdict of 'Not Proven' the pannel cannot be retried, no matter what new evidence may later come to light. Such a verdict is final. True, a slur is sometimes attached but better that than serve the substantial sentence endured by the subject of this book.

The Pannel: An accused person in solemn procedure.

Perjury: A person who swears or affirms falsely in giving evidence.

On Petition: In solemn procedure (see below) an arrested person appears in private before a Sheriff on the first day (excluding Saturdays and Sundays) after his arrest. The Procurator Fiscal presents a Petition to the Court narrating the nature of the charge and the Sheriff is asked to commit the prisoner for further examination or trial, with or without bail. The Crown, however, may still decide, subsequently, not to prosecute or to reduce the charge. Bail may be fixed at this appearance. There may also be the emission of a Judicial Declaration (this depends on the accused) and the charged person may be judicially examined before the Sheriff. This procedure (re-introduced under the Criminal Procedure (Scotland) Act, 1975) consists of the accused being asked certain questions by the Fiscal in order to ascertain if there is any special defence (see below) i.e., self defence, alibi, incrimination or consent (in charges of rape). The accused is advised that he is not required to answer any question but that if he opts so to do and at his trial puts points that could have been put at this early stage, the subsequent Jury could draw an adverse inference. He is always represented by a solicitor (unless he decides to act for himself) and can seek advice before answering any question. The proceedings are not on oath and everything said is recorded by tape and shorthand writer, later to be lodged and used at the trial. The Press is not allowed into the private Court and has no right to have access to the details of the charge occurring on the Petition.

Pleading Diets: In solemn matters were dispensed with as a result of the 1975 Criminal Procedure (Scotland) Act. The writer would prefer this Diet to be restored and sees little merit in its omission. It afforded an opportunity for the Pannel's solicitor and the Fiscal to get together ten days, at least, before trial.

Precognosce, Precognition (verb—pronounced Precognose): A precognition is a statement taken during the period of preparation of a case, by the prosecution or the defence, from victims and potential witnesses. They are precognosced to establish what evidence they would be likely to give in Court and, therefore, whether they should be called to testify.

Procurator Fiscal (informally Fiscal): Is responsible for all prosecutions in the lower Courts, under the direction of the Crown Office (see Lord Advocate, above). The Fiscal reports serious crimes to the Crown Office, who then (after consultation with the Advocates-Depute or Lord Advocate if necessary) decides whether or not to prosecute and if so, in which Court. Where a prosecution is directed by the Procurator Fiscal, he or one of his deputes handles the preparation of the case and conducts the prosecution in Court.

Reset: Consists in knowingly receiving articles taken by theft (see below), robbery, etc., and feloniously retaining them or being privy to their retention from the true owner. In other words, receiving or dealing in stolen goods, knowing them to be stolen and with the intention of keeping them from their rightful owner. The English term is *receiving*.

Royal Pardon: The exercise of the Queen's Prerogative of Mercy. Irrespective of what has occurred before the Courts of the land, the Monarch has the ultimate right to intervene and quash both conviction and sentence. She is, of course, advised by the Executive i.e., the Secretary of State in Scottish matters and the Home Secretary in those of England, Northern Ireland and Wales. Financial compensation would normally be paid out consequent upon such intervention—extremely rare as it is.

Sheriff Court: The Sheriff Courts, presided over by the Sheriffs, deal with most civil and criminal cases in Scotland. Sheriffs are appointed from among advocates and solicitors of at least ten years' standing. They may deal with minor cases on summary procedure or with more serious cases on solemn procedure (see below). The Sheriff Court does not, however, deal (a) with crimes committed outside the territorial limits of its jurisdiction, (b) with certain crimes—notably murder, treason, rape and incest—which must be tried in the High Court, or (c) with cases in which it is anticipated that a sentence of more than three years' imprisonment (the maximum a Sheriff can impose) will be appropriate in the event of a conviction. The Sheriff may also (in solemn procedure) remit an accused to the High Court for sentence, if he pleads guilty—or, on occasions, if he is found guilty at a trial—and the Sheriff feels that a longer sentence is called for than he can impose. In the Sheriff Court, the defence solicitor usually does the pleading himself, even in a jury trial.

Solemn Procedure: More serious crimes are tried either in the Sheriff Court or in the High Court of Justiciary before a Judge and Jury. In such instances the Sheriff has powers of imprisonment up to three years. The High Court Judge has all embracing powers of sentence unless restricted by Act of Parliament. Such solemn cases proceed by way of Indictment (see above) which is a formal document outlining the details of the charge, the List of Productions and Labels as well as the List of Witnesses to be advanced by the Crown.

Solatium: Damages given by way of reparation for injury to feelings. Damages in actions for personal injuries fall under the heads of (a) solatium, (b) patrimonial loss and (c) outlays and expenses. More fully the term applies to remuneration or reparation for the pain and suffering inflicted on a person in consequence of a delict against him. The word is from the Latin term 'solare'.

Special Defence: If an accused intends to maintain at his trial that he is not guilty of the charge because (a) he was elsewhere at the time of the offence and has an alibi, (b) he was acting in self defence (which is a complete answer to the charge), (c) that the crime was committed by someone else, (d) he was insane at the time but has now recovered his sanity, a special defence of alibi, self defence, impeachment/incrimination or insanity at the time must be lodged and intimated by him at least *ten* days before the date set for trial, thereby giving the Crown fair notice. This line of defence in no way imposes a burden of proof on the accused person or relieves the Crown of its overall burden of proving guilt beyond reasonable doubt. The exception is in special defence (d) when it is necessary for the Pannel to establish this defence beyond reasonable doubt. In the latter case, if successful, the verdict is acquittal by reason of insanity. In England the equivalent verdict would read 'Guilty but insane' which seems to be a misnomer.

Summary Procedure: Relates to relatively minor offences and are tried in our District and Sheriff Courts before either a magistrate or a Sheriff sitting alone and without a Jury. The maximum sentence is six months imprisonment, apart from a few exceptions. Under this procedure the accused is prosecuted on a Complaint signed by the Procurator Fiscal Depute, and not on an Indictment (solemn procedure).

Theft: Is the felonious taking and appropriation of property without the consent of the owner or custodier.

Hansard: Not a legal term but the printed reports of debates in Parliament. The founder was Luke Hansard (1752–1828) whose descendants continued to print them down to 1889.

Quorum: The minimum number of persons requiring to be present before any business may be transacted.